Teen Violence

Teen
Violence

Scott Barbour

$$\left[\begin{array}{c}\textbf{OPPOSING}\\\textbf{VIEWPOINTS}^{®}\\\text{DIGESTS}\end{array}\right]$$

Library of Congress Cataloging-in-Publication Data

Barbour, Scott, 1963–
    Teen violence / Scott Barbour
       p.   cm. — (Opposing viewpoints digests)
    Includes bibliographical references and index.
    Summary: Presents opposing viewpoints on the problem of teen violence, discussing how serious the problem may be, its causes, and ways to reduce it.
    ISBN 1-56510-865-5 (lib. bdg. : alk. paper). — ISBN 1-56510-864-7 (pbk. : alk. paper)
    1. Juvenile delinquency—United States—Juvenile literature.
2. Violence—United States—Juvenile literature. 3. Violence on television—United States—Juvenile literature. 4. Violent crimes—United States—Prevention—Juvenile literature. [1. Juvenile delinquency. 2. Violent Crimes. 3. Violence.] I. Title. II. Series.
HV9104.B339   1999
364.36'0973—dc21   98-36949
                                                  CIP
                                                    AC

©1999 by Greenhaven Press, Inc.
PO Box 289009, San Diego, CA 92198-9009

CONTENTS

FOREWORD

The only way in which a human being can make some approach to knowing the whole of a subject is by hearing what can be said about it by persons of every variety of opinion and studying all modes in which it can be looked at by every character of mind. No wise man ever acquired his wisdom in any mode but this.

—John Stuart Mill

Today, young adults are inundated with a wide variety of points of view on an equally wide spectrum of subjects. Often overshadowing traditional books and newspapers as forums for these views are a host of broadcast, print, and electronic media, including television news and entertainment programs, talk shows, and commercials; radio talk shows and call-in lines; movies, home videos, and compact discs; magazines and supermarket tabloids; and the increasingly popular and influential Internet.

For teenagers, this multiplicity of sources, ideas, and opinions can be both positive and negative. On the one hand, a wealth of useful, interesting, and enlightening information is readily available virtually at their fingertips, underscoring the need for teens to recognize and consider a wide range of views besides their own. As Mark Twain put it, "It were not best that we should all think alike; it is difference of opinion that makes horse races." On the other hand, the range of opinions on a given subject is often too wide to absorb and analyze easily. Trying to keep up with, sort out, and form personal opinions from such a barrage can be daunting for anyone, let alone young people who have not yet acquired effective critical judgment skills.

Moreover, to the task of evaluating this assortment of impersonal information, many teenagers bring firsthand experience of serious and emotionally charged social and health problems, including divorce, family violence, alcoholism and drug abuse, rape, unwanted pregnancy, the spread of AIDS, and eating disorders. Teens are often forced to deal with these problems before they are capable of objective opinion based on reason and judgment. All too often, teens' response to these deep personal issues is impulsive rather than carefully considered.

Greenhaven Press's Opposing Viewpoints Digests are designed to aid in examining important current issues in a way that develops critical thinking and evaluating skills. Each book presents thought-provoking argument and stimulating debate on a single issue. By examining an issue from many different points of view, readers come to realize its complexity and acknowledge the validity of opposing opinions. This insight is especially helpful in writing reports, research papers, and persuasive essays, when students must competently address common objections and controversies related to their topic. In addition, examination of the diverse mix of opinions in each volume challenges readers to question their own strongly held opinions and assumptions. While the point of such examination is not to change readers' minds, examining views that oppose their own will certainly deepen their own knowledge of the issue and help them realize exactly why they hold the opinion they do.

The Opposing Viewpoints Digests offer a number of unique features that sharpen young readers' critical thinking and reading skills. To assure an appropriate and consistent reading level for young adults, all essays in each volume are written by a single author. Each essay heavily quotes readable primary sources that are fully cited to allow for further research and documentation. Thus, primary sources are introduced in a context to enhance comprehension.

In addition, each volume includes extensive research tools. A section containing relevant source material includes interviews, excerpts from original research, and the opinions of prominent spokespersons. A "facts about" section allows students to peruse relevant facts and statistics; these statistics are also fully cited, allowing students to question and analyze the credibility of the source. Two bibliographies, one for young adults and one listing the author's sources, are also included; both are annotated to guide student research. Finally, a comprehensive index allows students to scan and locate content efficiently.

Greenhaven's Opposing Viewpoints Digests, like Greenhaven's higher level and critically acclaimed Opposing Viewpoints Series, have been developed around the concept that an awareness and appreciation for the complexity of seemingly simple issues is particularly important in a democratic society. In a democracy, the common good is often, and very appropriately, decided by open debate of widely varying views. As one of our democracy's greatest advocates, Thomas Jefferson, observed, "Difference of opinion leads to inquiry, and inquiry to truth." It is to this principle that Opposing Viewpoints Digests are dedicated.

What Causes Teen Violence?

Between September 1997 and May 1998, a series of shootings by teenagers at U.S. schools left at least thirteen people dead and more than forty injured. Three particular incidents provide a chilling picture of the problem:

On December 1, 1997, fourteen-year-old Michael Carneal arrived at Heath High School in West Paducah, Kentucky, armed with a pistol, two shotguns, two rifles, and seven hundred rounds of ammunition. He then shot and killed three students and wounded five others who were attending an early morning prayer meeting in the school's entrance hall.

On March 28, 1998, Andrew Golden, age eleven, and Mitchell Johnson, thirteen, ambushed students and teachers at Westside Middle School in Jonesboro, Arkansas. The boys, dressed in camouflage gear and armed with numerous guns—including three rifles and four pistols that they had stolen from Andrew's grandfather—lured teachers and students from the school buildings by setting off the fire alarm. Then they opened fire on the crowd from one hundred yards away, killing four students and one teacher and wounding eleven others.

On May 21, 1998, fifteen-year-old Kipland Kinkel, armed with three guns, opened fire in the crowded cafeteria of Thurston High School in Springfield, Oregon, killing two students and wounding twenty-three others. The bodies of his parents were later found shot to death in their family home.

These and similar incidents have increased the sense of urgency concerning the problem of teen violence in American society. Charles Patrick Ewing, a professor of law and psychiatry at the State University of New York at Buffalo, states that school shootings, although horrifying, are "just the tip of a much larger iceberg called juvenile violence."[1]

Indeed, according to the Federal Bureau of Investigation (FBI), between 1984 and 1994 the rate of violent juvenile crime increased 68 percent. The number of juveniles involved in murders increased from 1,037 in 1984 to 3,029 in 1994. More recently, the violent juvenile crime rate has declined slightly, decreasing 12 percent between 1994 and 1996. However, despite this positive sign, the 1996 rate remained 42 percent above the 1988 level, suggesting that the problem remains serious.

Politicians, public health officials, and citizens alike are alarmed about violent crimes committed by and against teens. In the wake of the school shootings of 1997 and 1998, many sought an explanation for why such killings were taking place. Following the Jonesboro, Arkansas, shooting, Sandy Grady, a columnist for the *Philadelphia Daily News*, described the pictures of the victims. She wrote, "The faces of the dead ask, 'Why?' The answers don't come easy."[2] Indeed, whether examining one specific act of violence or the problem as a whole, the answer to the question "Why?" is far from simple.

Violent Crime Arrest Rates

Arrests per 100,000 juveniles ages 10–17

Source: Office of Juvenile Justice and Delinquency Prevention

Nature Versus Nurture

Various answers are presented in response to the question of what causes teen violence. Behind all of them lies an ongoing theoretical debate over "nature versus nurture." Those who attribute the causes to nature contend that certain people are born with a tendency to be violent due to their genetic makeup or other biological factors, such as brain chemicals or neurological damage. Some scientists point to biology to explain why males are more likely to be violent than females. Researchers have discovered that men with high levels of the hormone testosterone are more aggressive than those with relatively low levels. This finding leads them to suggest that testosterone—a male hormone—may account for the fact that males commit the vast majority of violent crimes.

Other researchers focus on the role of genetics in causing violent behavior. Byron M. Roth, a psychology professor at Dowling College, writes, "Recent research provides considerable support for the idea . . . that criminals are born rather than made; genes appear to count far more than upbringing."[3] Tom Jacobson, a family friend of the Kinkels, expressed this view when he said of the fifteen-year-old shooter in Springfield, Oregon, "Young Kip was just a bad seed."[4]

On the other hand, those who favor nurture in the nature versus nurture debate believe violent behavior is nurtured by the environment; that is, children and teens are taught to be violent by aspects of the culture in which they live. For example, in American society boys are taught to be physically assertive and competitive. Some experts stress this social conditioning, rather than testosterone, as one factor behind the higher rate of violent crime among males.

The nature versus nurture debate is largely a matter of degrees or emphasis. Few people believe that genes or other biological factors are entirely responsible for violence. A person may have a genetic predisposition, or tendency, toward violence, but that alone is not enough to cause them to act in violent ways. In addition to a genetic predisposition, many sociologists believe that certain conditions in the environment are necessary to trigger the violence. After describing the extensive research supporting the theory that nature is more important than nurture, Roth states:

> None of the above should be interpreted to mean that a person is destined by his genes to a life of crime. . . . Genes do not program individual behavior in a vacuum; ecological factors clearly play a role in what sort of genetic predispositions are expressed in . . . behavior. In other words, some environments are more conducive than others for the expression of criminal traits.[5]

While a great deal of research is being done on the contribution that genes and other biological influences make to violence, most commentators focus on the environmental factors that are suspected of nurturing violent behavior among teens.

Guns

In the wake of the school shootings of 1997 and 1998, many people argued that the widespread availability of guns in the United States contributes heavily to the problem of teen violence. They pointed out that both of the perpetrators in the Jonesboro shooting were hunters who had been taught to use guns at a very early age. In searching for the answer to why the Jonesboro shooting occurred, Sandy Grady wrote, "Maybe it will come down to guns. Usually does. Hard to imagine the Jonesboro, Ark., kid murders happening any place but America, where weaponry is ubiquitous as Big Macs."[6]

To bolster their case, critics of America's "gun culture" point out that the rate of gun-related juvenile homicide tripled between 1984 and 1994 while the rate of non–gun-related juvenile homicide remained relatively stable. Gun violence hits African American teenagers especially hard; gun-related homicide is the leading cause of death for black males between the ages of fifteen and nineteen.

However, critics are quick to discount the role of guns in causing teen violence. They argue that many teens are hunters and are proficient with guns, and the vast majority do not commit gun homicide. As stated by Timothy Wheeler, the director of Doctors for Responsible Gun Ownership,

> If the blame lay solely with "gun culture," one should expect this sort of violence to have happened all along in American history. Generations of American youths have grown up around guns without feeling at all compelled to commit multiple murder. To the contrary, most young people who train today in the shooting sports learn excellence and discipline as they do in any sport.[7]

Personal Responsibility

Those who believe that guns are not the problem argue that rather than blaming guns, society should focus on the forces that compel teens to pick up guns and use them against other people. Many conservatives contend that teens who commit violent crimes do so because they lack a sense of personal responsibility. Examining the question of what causes juvenile crime, Morgan Reynolds, the director of the Criminal Justice Center at the National Center for Policy Analysis, states:

> What causes crime? We don't need a lot of sociological mumbo-jumbo to answer this question. The guilty criminal does! He (93 percent of offenders are male) is a free moral agent who, confronted with a choice between right and wrong, chooses to do wrong, even if only for a brief period in his life. He refuses to respect the rights of others to be secure in their lives and possessions.[8]

Morgan contends that violent teens choose to commit violence because they are devoid of a sense of morality and empathy for the pain and suffering of others: "More youths than ever are effectively growing up as barbarians, failing to adopt the minimum ethics required for peaceful cooperation."[9]

The Role of Parents

Social analysts offer theories about why today's teens lack the values that would prevent them from committing crime, such as respect for others, empathy, and a sense of right and wrong. Parents are frequently blamed for failing to teach their children the importance of restraint. In response to the Kip Kinkel shooting in Springfield, Oregon, columnist Georgie Anne Geyer argued that the cause of such violence is not guns, but the failure of parents to discipline their children:

> Is this not where common sense tells us it all starts, with what is in effect an enormous vacuum of authority in this country caused by . . . the mothers and fathers who are not willing to do what is necessary to inculcate a moral control within children when they are young?[10]

However, even the children of good parents often get into trouble. For example, Kip Kinkel reportedly had dedicated parents who were widely respected members of their community. Tom Jacobson, the Kinkels' family friend, said that in the two years prior to the shooting, Kip was having behavioral problems, but his parents tried to help him. "They did everything possible with that boy," he stated. "As parents, they just kept trying."[11]

Family Breakdown

Not all troubled teens like Kip have the support of two parents. The number of single-mother families has increased dramatically since the mid-1970s. Moreover, half of all marriages in America end in divorce. Many conservatives cite these trends as evidence of the breakdown of the traditional two-parent family. As a result of this change in the family structure, these social critics maintain, young boys are left without the support and discipline of fathers, who have traditionally fulfilled the role of shaping boys into mature, responsible, self-restrained, empathetic young men.

The absence of fathers is believed to contribute directly to the problem of teen violence. The shooting in Jonesboro would seem to lend support to this theory. Reporters noted that the parents of Mitchell Johnson, one of the shooters, had divorced in 1994, four years prior to the attack. Mitchell had been living with his mother since that time. Following the divorce, according to relatives, he became temperamental and developed an interest in gangs. After the Jonesboro shooting, forensic psychologist Shawn Johnston stated, "This is the price we are paying as a society for the number of fathers who have bailed out on their children. The extent to which fathers have abandoned socializing the young male animal is just mind-boggling."[12]

The belief that teen violence stems from the growing number of single-parent families is not universally shared. While in most cases a two-parent family is probably more beneficial for children, many people are quick to insist that single mothers are capable of raising crime-free sons. As columnist Clarence Page writes, "It is not the quantity of parents but the quality of parenting that counts."[13]

Media Violence

Media violence is also blamed for contributing to teen violence. Many media critics contend that exposure to violence on television and in movies, music, and video games promotes violence in at least two ways. First, it desensitizes teens to the pain and suffering caused by real-world violence. Second, it sends the message that violence is an effective way to solve problems. Describing the effects of television, Margot Prior, a professor of clinical psychology, writes:

> Children who watch violent episodes show increased likelihood of behaving aggressively after the viewing, and there are cumulative effects of a diet of violence

over time. Heavy consumers grow up to be more aggressive than light consumers.[14]

This thesis was lent some validity when Michael Carneal, the fourteen-year-old responsible for the school shooting in West Paducah, Kentucky, claimed that he was inspired to commit the shooting by a violent scene in the movie *The Basketball Diaries*. In that scene, the main character of the film fantasizes about opening fire on a classroom full of students with a shotgun.

Not everyone, however, sees a cause-and-effect relationship between media violence and real-world teen violence. Few commentators defend media violence as a constructive influence on children and teens, yet many, like Kevin Durkin, an associate professor of psychology at the University of Western Australia, fail to see evidence of a connection to real-world violence. Durkin writes, "There is no scientific basis for assuming [media violence] plays a major role in the development of aggression."[15] These skeptics believe that while a few particular acts of teen violence may mimic violence depicted in the media, the cause of the violence lies elsewhere. For example, after the West Paducah shooting, school principal Bill Bond stated that Michael Carneal, the shooter, was a physically small, emotionally immature boy who "had been teased all his life" and "just struck out in anger at the world."[16] Although he may have imitated an act of media violence, the underlying cause of the violence may have been Carneal's feelings of anger and frustration stemming from his inability to fit in with peers.

Crazy Murders

In attempting to understand the school shootings, it is tempting to isolate one explanation, such as media violence or guns. Most analysts, however, are aware that multiple factors combine to produce an event like the West Paducah, Jonesboro, and Springfield attacks. Charles Patrick Ewing refers to such shootings as "crazy murders." Patrick O'Neill, a staff writer for the *Portland Oregonian* newspaper, summarizes Ewing's description of such a murder:

A crazy murder has no obvious motive. Not robbery. Not rape. Not even revenge for a specific wrong. There's virtually no chance the killer will get away. A mass shooting is like a storm of circumstance . . . in which elements swirl together until they align with a youngster's finger on the trigger of a gun.

The elements include a boy's background and psychological makeup, the availability of a gun, the tensions and disappointments of a given day.[17]

Ewing contends that teens who commit such murders are likely to have common characteristics and engage in similar behaviors, such as committing violence against animals, an interest in setting fires or making bombs, making threats to harm other people, and a disregard for other people's rights.

The school shootings of 1997 and 1998 seem to conform to Ewing's description of crazy murders. In the West Paducah, Jonesboro, and Springfield shootings, a combination of circumstances—rather than one single cause—appear to have fed into each killer's decision to take guns to school and shoot people. While not all of the shooters shared all of the characteristics listed by O'Neill, they each possessed some of them. All of the shooters had an interest in weapons. Kip Kinkel enjoyed torturing animals, collecting guns, and building bombs. He was voted "most likely to start World War III" by his classmates in middle school.

In all three cases, threats or warnings were made prior to the shootings. Kip Kinkel joked about killing people. Michael Carneal had previously talked about shooting classmates and, the week prior to the shooting, warned people that "something big" was going to happen. Mitchell Johnson also warned students prior to the shooting in Jonesboro, saying, "Tomorrow you will find out if you live or die."[18]

In addition, all of the boys were having psychological, emotional, or social problems at the time of the shootings. Various factors may have contributed to Mitchell Johnson's personal problems.

Some juvenile murderers seem to defy easy explanation. Kipland Kinkel, who shot his parents and two classmates, came from a devoted and caring two-parent family.

According to reports, he may have been sexually molested between the ages of six and seven. In addition, as previously noted, he began to exhibit behavioral problems following his parents' divorce in 1994. Finally, he was rejected by a girl in the days leading up to the shooting. Similarly, on the day prior to the Springfield shooting, Kip Kinkel was suspended from school for possessing a stolen gun.

Another factor that links all of the school shootings is that all of the shooters were to some degree alienated from their peers. Referring to the West Paducah, Jonesboro, Springfield, and other school shootings, Gordon Witkin and his colleagues at *U.S. News & World Report*, write:

Many of the reputed perpetrators apparently felt like outsiders. They were not star athletes or school leaders but kids who were out of the mainstream—unhappy, searching for their place, and suffering ridicule. . . . Kinkel was angry at being teased by older students. Johnson from Jonesboro was known as a bully and a braggart, but he was also teased for being fat. . . . Michael Carneal . . . was a fidgety, bespectacled young man sometimes described by peers as a "dweeb."[19]

A sense of alienation is a common aspect of adolescence, and most teenagers who experience teasing do not resort to extreme violence. But it seems likely that the experience of being rejected by fellow students contributed to the emotional instability that led to each shooter's decision to lash out.

These and other aspects of the shootings suggest that Ewing's characterization of them as crazy murders is correct. No single cause can be pinned down. In each case, a combination of events, past and present, together with the teens' individual temperament and the availability of guns, culminated in tragedy.

Inner-City Violence

The school shootings of 1997 and 1998 attracted a great deal of attention largely because they took place in predominately white, suburban, middle-class areas. According to Michael Flynn, however, a psychologist at John Jay College in New York, "This stuff's been happening in the inner city for 10 years, and for many of the same reasons. Has it taken middle-class kids' shooting each other to realize something is wrong?"[20]

Statistics suggest that violence is indeed a larger problem for inner-city minority teens than white teens. Although

African Americans made up 15 percent of the U.S. population in 1996, they comprised about one-half of arrests for violent juvenile crime, according to FBI statistics. However, minorities are not only arrested in disproportionate numbers, they are also much more likely to be victimized by violent crime. In 1994 African American youths were six times more likely than whites to be murdered.

The extent of violence in the inner city was demonstrated by a survey conducted by Mark Spellmann and Gerald Landsberg of the New York University School of Social Work. Spellmann and Landsberg interviewed 850 students in the sixth, seventh, and eighth grades at a school in Brooklyn, New York, about their experience with violence. Kim Nauer, the senior editor of *City Limits* magazine, reports the results of the study:

> Thirty-three percent of the children claimed to have "badly beat" someone in the previous four months. Twenty-six percent said they had carried a weapon at least once during that period. Fifteen percent claimed to have threatened someone with a weapon. Fifteen percent claimed to have robbed someone and 13 percent said they had been arrested.[21]

These statistics reveal that violence is a pervasive part of life in the inner city.

Causes of Inner-City Violence

As psychologist Michael Flynn suggests, many of the causes of teen violence in the inner cities are likely to be the same as those in the white suburbs. However, some believe that conditions specific to urban areas make violence more likely to occur there than in other areas. One study suggests that exposure to large amounts of violence is itself a cause of violence in the inner cities. Arlene Stiffman, an associate professor at the George Warren School of Social Work, surveyed 797 youths in St. Louis, Missouri, and found that those teens who were exposed to large doses of violence were more likely to behave violently. Stiffman concludes:

> Our study demonstrates a direct link between teen-
> agers' exposure to violence and their own violent behav-
> iors. The more violence that the youths had been
> exposed to, the more likely they were to be violent
> themselves.[22]

According to Stiffman, urban youths who are exposed to violence are more likely to be violent because they "see no hope
for the future, feel suicidal, and do not know how to escape
from the violence except by being violent themselves or
numbing themselves with drugs or alcohol."[23]

Others point out that the number of single-mother families
is especially high among inner-city minorities: Sixty-eight
percent of African American babies are born to single mothers. The absence of fathers and other adult male role models
is widely cited as a major contributor to the problem of violent juvenile crime in the inner city.

Economic and social conditions in the inner city are also
cited as contributors to violence among teens. Commentators
contend that poverty, unemployment, and deteriorating social
institutions (such as schools and churches) create a sense of
helplessness and despair in young people. Teens in this type of
environment often perceive a lack of legitimate job opportunities or hope for the future. Such teens may then be lured
into membership in a gang. As James Alan Fox, dean of the
College of Criminal Justice at Northeastern University, states,

> It is clear that too many teenagers in this country, par-
> ticularly those in urban areas, are plagued with idleness
> and even hopelessness. A growing number of teens and
> preteens see few feasible or attractive alternatives to
> violence, drug use, and gang membership.[24]

Gangs, Drugs, and Guns

Although not all gangs are violent, violence in the inner cities
often goes hand in hand with gang activity. A survey of one
thousand youths in the Rochester, New York, public schools,

conducted by the Office of Juvenile Justice and Delinquency Prevention (OJJDP), revealed the connection between gangs and youth violence. Thirty percent of the youths surveyed had been involved in a gang. That 30 percent was responsible for 68 percent of the violent crimes committed by the entire group. In other words, gang members were responsible for more than twice their share of violent crime.

Others point to the role of the drug trade in causing teen violence in the inner cities. When crack cocaine arrived in urban centers in the early 1980s, many minority teens became involved in dealing the drug. The drug trade was attractive to these youths because legitimate forms of employment were scarce and because large sums of money could be made due to the high demand for the highly addictive substance. As more and more teens joined the lucrative enterprise, they began to carry—and to use—guns. As Alfred Blumstein of Carnegie Mellon University explains,

> The surge in violent juvenile crime [between 1985 and 1992] coincided with an increase in drug arrests, which rose particularly among nonwhites in urban areas. . . . To meet the growth in demand for crack cocaine, the drug industry had recruited young sellers, primarily nonwhite youths, many of whom saw this as their only viable economic activity. . . . As more juveniles were recruited to sell crack, they armed themselves with guns.[25]

According to Blumstein, the growth of the crack trade led directly to an increase in gun-related violence among minorities in the inner cities.

No Single Cause

Whether it occurs in the ghettos of the inner cities or the schoolyards of middle-class suburbs, violence committed by teens cannot be attributed to a single cause. The most that can be said with certainty is that any one act of teen violence is the result of a complex interplay of forces, including the teen's emotional and psychological state, the circumstances of his or her life, and the influence of the culture at large. The essays that follow debate some of the potential causes of teen violence. They also examine the prevalence of teen violence in America and offer debate on how to bring this problem under control.

1. Quoted in Patrick O'Neill, "Teen Killers Do Fit a Pattern, Experts Say," *San Diego Union-Tribune*, May 31, 1998, p. G-4.

2. Sandy Grady, "The Questions After Jonesboro," *San Diego Union-Tribune*, March 27, 1998, p. B-10.

3. Byron M. Roth, "Crime and Child-Rearing: What Can Public Policy Do?" *Current*, January 1997, p. 3.

4. Quoted in Patricia King and Andrew Murr, "A Son Who Spun Out of Control," *Newsweek*, June 1, 1998, p. 33.

5. Roth, "Crime and Child-Rearing," p. 6.

6. Grady, "The Questions After Jonesboro," p. B-10.

7. Timothy Wheeler, "Blaming the Guns," *Washington Times*, June 2, 1998. On-line. Internet. Available http://www.claremont.org/wheeler2.htm.

8. Morgan Reynolds, "Abolish the Juvenile Justice System?" *Intellectual Ammunition*, November/December 1996. On-line. Internet. Available http://www.heartland.org/03nvdc96.htm.

9. Reynolds, "Abolish the Juvenile Justice System?"

10. Georgie Anne Geyer, "'Gun-Crazy,' Yes, But the Causes of Teen Shootings Run Much Deeper," *San Diego Union-Tribune*, May 31, 1998, p. G-4.

11. Quoted in William Claiborne, "Bombs Found in Ore. Teen's Home," *Washington Post*, May 23, 1998, p. A-1. On-line. Internet. Available http://www.washingtonpost.com/wp-srv/national/lonterm/juvmurders/stories/bombs.htm.

12. Quoted in Elizabeth Kastor, "What Makes Children Kill?" *Washington Post*, March 27, 1998, p. C-1.

13. Clarence Page, "Consensus Reflects a Changing 'Family,'" *Liberal Opinion Week*, August 8, 1994, p. 8.

14. Margot Prior, speech presented at the Stories We Tell Our Children Conference in Melbourne, Australia, August 1994. On-line. Internet. Available http://cii2.cochran.com/mnet/eng/issues/violence/resource/docs/C-aba-ag.htm.

15. Kevin Durkin, "Chasing the Effects of Media Violence," *ABA Update: Newsletter of the Australian Broadcasting Authority*, March 1995. On-line. Internet. Available http://www.screen.com/mnet/eng/issues/violence/resource/articles/chasefx.htm.

16. Quoted in "Who Is Michael Carneal?" CNN Interactive, December 3, 1997. On-line. Internet. Available http://www.cnn.com/US/9712/03/school.shooting.pm/.

17. O'Neill, "Teen Killers Do Fit a Pattern, Experts Say," p. G-4.

18. Quoted in John Kifner, "From Wild Talk and Friendship to Five Deaths in a Schoolyard," *New York Times*, March 29, 1998, p. A-1.

19. Gordon Witkin et al., "Again," *U.S. News & World Report*, June 1, 1998.

20. Quoted in King and Murr, "A Son Who Spun Out of Control," p. 33.

21. Kim Nauer, "Motive and Opportunity," *City Limits*, December 1995, p. 16.

22. Quoted in "Violence Triggers a Vicious Cycle," *USA Today*, December 1995.

23. Quoted in "Violence Triggers a Vicious Cycle," *USA Today*.

24. James Alan Fox, "Should the Federal Government Have a Major Role in Reducing Juvenile Crime? Pro," *Congressional Digest*, August/September 1996, p. 206.

25. Alfred Blumstein, *Youth Violence, Guns, and Illicit Drug Markets*. Washington, D.C.: National Institute of Justice, June 1996.

CHAPTER 1

How Serious Is the Problem of Teen Violence?

"Every day seems to bring fresh news of mayhem at the hands of the nation's young people."

Teen Violence Is a Serious Problem

Four teenagers are caught on a surveillance video camera robbing a market in Harrisburg, Pennsylvania. As the owner stands with his hands raised, one of the teens, a fourteen-year-old, shoots him in the head.

Five teenagers from Florida and Kentucky who consider themselves vampires are charged with beating one of the teens' parents to death.

A fourteen-year-old boy opens fire after a prayer meeting at a Kentucky high school, killing two girls and wounding six other students.

A seventeen-year-old San Diego boy is beaten to death by three other teens in a dispute over a skateboard.

In Los Angeles a six-year-old boy is killed by a bullet to the head, another innocent bystander caught in the crossfire of a teenage gang shooting.

These are just a few of the stories that have appeared on the front pages of America's newspapers as testimony to the rise of senseless brutality committed by teenagers. Reports such as these have become so common that they have nearly lost their ability to shock. Every day seems to bring fresh news of mayhem at the hands of the nation's young people. As one team of researchers states, "Compared to adolescents in other countries,

Students embrace an adult in the aftermath of shootings at their Paducah, Kentucky, high school. The increasing number of such incidents suggests that teens are becoming more violent.

American teens exhibit alarmingly high rates of violence."[1] What's worse, they resort to violence with an easy, casual attitude, revealing that they are indifferent to the pain and suffering that result from their vicious acts.

Statistics Reveal a Crisis

The popular perception that teen violence is on the upswing is supported by statistics. The Office of Juvenile Justice and Delinquency Prevention (OJJDP), a division of the U.S. Department of Justice, has reported that cases of violent crime committed by juveniles have risen dramatically. Between 1985 and 1994, according to the OJJDP, juvenile homicide increased 144 percent, juvenile rape increased 25 percent, and cases of aggravated assault by juveniles increased 134 percent.

As these numbers suggest, juveniles commit a large proportion of America's violent crime. According to the Federal

Bureau of Investigation (FBI), juveniles made up 19 percent of all violent crime arrests in 1996. Juveniles are responsible for 8 percent of murders, 12 percent of forcible rapes, 18 percent of robberies, and 12 percent of aggravated assaults cleared (solved) by law enforcement, the FBI reports.

And it's not just the boys who are engaging in violent behavior. Girls are increasingly involved in violent crime, including gang violence. According to the OJJDP, 15 percent of juveniles arrested for violent crime are female. The FBI adds that the number of female juveniles arrested for violent crime increased 25 percent between 1992 and 1996.

Some people try to downplay the seriousness of the youth violence problem by pointing out that the rates of violent juvenile crime actually decreased in 1995 and 1996. While this is certainly welcome news, it masks the fact that the overall trend is an escalation of teen violence over the past ten years. Despite the recent dip, the number of juvenile arrests for violent crime in 1996 was still 60 percent above the 1987 level. It would be foolish to point to the recent decline in juvenile crime rates as a sign that the problem of teen violence is subsiding.

Today's Teens Are More Callous

While the number of violent crimes committed by juveniles has increased, the nature of the crimes has also changed. The nonchalance with which many of today's teenagers shoot rival gang members and torture their robbery and rape victims is chilling. John J. DiIulio Jr., a scholar at the Brookings Institution, a public-policy think tank, writes that "the kids doing the violent crimes are more impulsively violent and remorseless than ever."[2]

In an article in *Newsweek*, reporter Michele Ingrassia provides an example of the callousness and remorselessness of today's violent teens. She describes in detail how six teenage gang members in Houston brutally raped and murdered two teenage girls who had taken a shortcut through the woods:

The nude bodies of the girls were found four days later; they had been raped repeatedly and strangled, one with a belt, the other with shoelaces. It was not enough. "To ensure that both of them were dead," a police spokesman said, "the suspects stood on the girls' necks."[3]

Any civilized person would be appalled at the thought of such brutality. And anyone with the slightest moral sense would feel extreme remorse at having taken part in it. However, upon hearing that he would be charged with murder in the case, one of the boys displayed the lack of conscience that has become so prevalent among today's violent youths. He replied, "Hey, great! We've hit the big time!"[4] This is just one of countless examples of cold-bloodedness that are featured on the front pages of newspapers and on the evening news almost daily in America.

DiIulio characterizes these callous teens as "juvenile super-predators who maim and murder without remorse or fear."[5] Clearly the fault lies with society for failing to teach children right from wrong. Adults are not providing young people with the moral guidance they need to develop concern for the well-being of others. As DiIulio explains,

What I have termed juvenile "super-predators" are born of abject "moral poverty," which I define as the poverty of being without loving, capable, responsible adults who teach you right from wrong. It is the poverty of being without parents, guardians, relatives, friends, teachers, coaches, clergy and others who habituate you to feel joy at others' joy, pain at others' pain, happiness when you do right, remorse when you do wrong. It is the poverty of growing up in the virtual absence of people who teach these lessons by their own everyday example, and who insist that you follow suit and behave accordingly.[6]

Society's failure to teach children right from wrong not only deprives young people of the basic human need to enjoy compassion and empathy, it also puts the social fabric at risk.

The Violence Will Get Worse

The number of super-predators is expected to increase dramatically in the next ten to twenty years as the number of teenagers in the population increases. According to the U.S. Census Bureau, the number of males between fifteen and nineteen will reach 11.5 million in 2010, up from 9.2 million in 1990. This increase in the number of teenage boys means "our nation faces the grim prospect of a future wave of juvenile violence that may make the 1990s look like 'the good old days,'"[7] writes James Alan Fox, dean of the College of Criminal Justice at Northeastern University.

Faced with this impending wave of violent juvenile crime, policy makers must take action to protect society from the young predators in our midst. Ordinary citizens have the right to live their lives free from the threat that they or their loved ones will be victimized by youths who lack the values that hold society together.

1. Barbara Tatem Kelley et al., *Epidemiology of Serious Violence*. Washington, DC: Office of Juvenile Justice and Delinquency Prevention, June 1997.

2. Senate, John J. DiIulio Jr., speaking before the Subcommittee on Youth Violence, February 28, 1996.

3. Michele Ingrassia, "'Life Means Nothing,'" *Newsweek*, July 19, 1993, p. 16.

4. Quoted in Ingrassia, "'Life Means Nothing,'" p. 17.

5. John J. DiIulio Jr., "Defining Criminality Up," *Wall Street Journal*, July 3, 1996.

6. Senate, DiIulio.

7. James Alan Fox, "Should the Federal Government Have a Major Role in Reducing Juvenile Crime? Pro," *Congressional Digest*, August/September 1996, p. 210.

"Children run a higher risk of being the victims than the perpetrators of violence."

The Problem of Teen Violence Has Been Exaggerated

The media and politicians love to wring their hands about teen violence. Consequently, the public has been led to believe the problem is worse than it actually is. In 1994 a Gallup poll found that American adults believed that youths were responsible for 43 percent of violent crimes in the United States. In fact, young people were responsible for only 13 percent of such crimes that year.

The fuss over teen violence does have some basis in fact. Statistics indicate that teenagers are committing a significant amount of violence. Moreover, for most of the past decade the rate of teen violence has been rising. However, rather than accept the hysterical news reporting and get-tough-on-crime political rhetoric that is so prevalent these days, it would be prudent to put this issue into perspective. As stated by the Children's Defense Fund, a child advocacy organization,

> While no amount of brutality by or against young people can be tolerated, honest examinations of demographics, crime trends, and the potential of prevention efforts do *not* indicate that today's young children should be objects of fear tomorrow.[1]

Statistics in Perspective

The rates of violent juvenile crime did increase between 1985 and 1994. According to the Office of Juvenile Justice and Delinquency Prevention (OJJDP), the number of juvenile arrests for violent crimes increased 98 percent between 1985 and 1994. However, more recent statistics suggest that violence is actually declining. Juvenile violent crime arrests decreased 3 percent in 1995 and 6 percent in 1996. More specifically, juvenile murder arrests declined 14 percent in 1995 and another 14 percent in 1996. This news disproves the dramatic but overblown claim that teens are becoming more violent and are devolving into a subhuman species of cold-blooded criminals who are capable of killing without pity or remorse.

In addition, the impression created by the media that vast numbers of teens are committing violence is false. According to the Federal Bureau of Investigation (FBI), only 1 in 220 (fewer than 0.5 percent) of persons between the ages of ten and seventeen was arrested for a violent crime in 1996. This number refutes the claim that society is being overrun by hordes of violent youths.

Adults Commit Most Violent Crimes

In truth, it is adults who commit the vast majority of violent crimes. The FBI reports that juveniles made up 19 percent of those arrested for violent crime in 1996. Those who promote the hysteria over juvenile crime point to this number as evidence that youth violence is pervasive. However, the obvious flip side to this statistic is that the remaining 81 percent of those arrested for violent crime are adults. This clearly shows that violent crime is primarily an adult problem.

Not only do adults commit most violent crimes, they are also the perpetrators of most crimes against young people. According to the U.S. Department of Justice, 60 percent of murdered teens are killed by adults, not other teens. In fact, young people run a higher risk of being the victims than the perpetrators of violence. As the Children's Defense Fund points out, "Children and youths are 10 times more likely to be victims *of* violence than to be arrested *for* violence."[2] The fund reports that in 1994, 1.6 million American teens were the victims of violent crimes (other than murder or abuse by family members and caretakers). These numbers suggest that the focus on teen violence is misplaced. Violence *is* a problem in the United States. But rather than being the cause of violence, teenagers are more often the victims of violence, and usually that violence is committed by adults.

Poverty Is the Real Problem

The focus on teen violence is misplaced for another reason. To the extent that youth violence persists, it is a symptom of a much larger and pervasive problem: poverty. According to Mike Males, the author of *The Scapegoat Generation: America's War on Adolescents*, experts agree that poverty is a root cause of violence. He writes, "While most impoverished people are not violent, there is no question among criminologists that the stresses of poverty are associated with much higher violent crime levels among all races and ages."[3]

Males compared the rate of teen violence in the United States with that of nineteen other industrialized countries. He concluded that the higher rate of youth violence found in America could be attributed to the higher rate of poverty in the United States:

> The major factor buried in teen-violence stories and rarely generating any remedies, is poverty. The biggest differences between the U.S. and the 19 other relatively peaceful industrial nations [studied] are youth poverty and extreme disparities in income between rich and poor. . . . The U.S. raises three to eight times more children in poverty than other Western nations. . . .
>
> In 1993, 40 million Americans lived below the official poverty line. . . . Half of these are children, and six in ten are nonwhite.[4]

Males contends that if poverty is taken into account in calculating the statistics, "the phenomenon of 'teenage violence' disappears: Adjusted for poverty, 13- to 19-year-olds have almost the same crime rate as people in their 40s, and have a crime rate well below those in their 20s and 30s."[5]

Further proof that poverty is the real problem can be seen in the fact that minority teens—who are more likely to live in poverty—experience more violence that white youths. First, nonwhite youths are much more likely to be arrested for violent crimes. In 1994, according to the OJJDP, juvenile homicide offenders were 61 percent African American and 36 percent white. More important, nonwhite teens are much more likely to be victimized by violence. The OJJDP reports that in 1994 African American juveniles were six times more likely to be murdered than white juveniles.

One final statistic speaks volumes about the plight of African American youths in America: Gun-related homicide is the leading cause of death among African-American teens between fifteen and nineteen. Males argues that if poverty is factored in when calculating the statistics on youth violence, it is clear that poverty is responsible for the higher rate of violence among minority teens: "If one adjusts the racial crime rate for the number of individuals living in extreme poverty, non-whites have a crime rate similar to that of whites at every age level."[6]

If teen violence is a relatively insignificant problem when compared to adult violence and poverty, why have the media and politicians seized upon it as one of today's burning issues? The tendency to focus on teen violence serves at least two purposes. First, it allows politicians to divert the public's attention from their failure to solve society's real problems—including poverty and violence against children. Second, it allows adults to justify their failure to take responsibility for the well-being of the nation's young people. As stated by Barbara Ehrenreich in *Time* magazine, "The more we convince ourselves that errant children are subhuman predators, the easier it gets to deny all children in poverty the resources and nurture they need. If they are the predators, we must be the vulnerable prey."[7]

It's time to stop fearing the young and start providing them with the support they need to navigate the minefields of childhood and adolescence.

1. Children's Defense Fund, *The State of America's Children: Yearbook 1997.* Washington, DC: Children's Defense Fund, 1997, p. 61.

2. Children's Defense Fund, *The State of America's Children*, p. 61.

3. Mike Males, "Wild in Deceit," *Extra!* March/April 1996, p. 9.

4. Males, "Wild in Deceit," p. 9.

5. Males, "Wild in Deceit," p. 9.

6. Males, "Wild in Deceit," p. 9.

7. Barbara Ehrenreich, "Oh, Grow Up!" *Time*, November 4, 1996, p. 100.

CHAPTER 2

What Causes Teen Violence?

"Fatherless boys are more apt to join gangs and commit violent crimes."

The Breakdown of the Family Causes Teen Violence

It would be simplistic to attribute all the violence committed by teenagers to one cause. However, it is clear that the breakdown of the traditional family structure that has occurred in recent decades is a major contributor to this problem. More and more children are being raised in homes that lack the economic and emotional stability that only an intact two-parent family can provide. The consequences of this trend are far-reaching. Experts agree that being raised in a single-parent home increases children's risk for a variety of problems, including poverty, poor educational performance, emotional problems—and violent behavior.

Social scientists have established that children raised in a single-parent family are more likely to commit violent crime. Barbara Dafoe Whitehead, a social historian and the author of a comprehensive article describing the harms of single-parent families, writes,

> Nationally, more than 70 percent of all juveniles in state reform institutions come from fatherless homes. . . . Boys from single-mother homes are significantly more

likely than others to commit crimes and to wind up in
the juvenile justice, court, and penitentiary systems.[1]

In addition, research indicates that neighborhoods with a
higher proportion of single-parent households have higher
rates of violent crime. This evidence suggests that Americans
have underestimated the important role the traditional family
structure plays in ensuring the well-being of the nation's children and society at large.

Divorce and Unwed Parenthood

In order to appreciate the impact of the changing family structure on the problem of teenage violence, it is necessary to understand why the number of single-parent families has increased.
The answer lies in the changing social values and norms
regarding divorce and unwed parenthood. Prior to the 1970s
the belief that a stable, two-parent family was essential for a
child's well-being was widely shared. When a marriage turned
bad, parents were expected to sacrifice their personal happiness
and weather the marital storm for the sake of the children.
There was general agreement that it was better for children to
have two parents, even if the marriage was less than ideal.

In the mid-1970s, however, the prevailing view of the
importance of an intact family began to shift. Parents' happiness began to take precedence over that of their children.
Divorce became a socially acceptable alternative to an unhappy marriage. Today, while no one would expect a woman to
remain in an abusive marriage (in such a case divorce is in the
children's best interest as well as the adults'), too many marriages are dissolved simply because they have become difficult,
inconvenient, or constraining. Consequently, 50 percent of
marriages in the United States today end in divorce.

The effects of divorce can be traumatic. Children of divorce
are put through a chaotic and distressing ordeal as they are
forced to accept the dissolution of their family—their source
of security, love, and support—and adjust to a new family

arrangement. Additionally, their new lives are often unstable, involving shared custody arrangements, stepparents and stepsiblings, and their parents' new romantic partners. All of this instability can undermine a child's sense of security and belonging, which in turn can lead to various problems, including poor school performance, depression, and delinquent behavior.

Along with divorce, unwed pregnancy and childbirth have also become more socially acceptable. Prior to the 1970s, if a young girl or woman became pregnant outside of marriage, she was subjected to censure by the community. If a marriage could not be arranged, her child was branded "illegitimate."

Rates of violent juvenile crime are highest in neighborhoods where single-parent families are concentrated.

Since the 1970s the stigma associated with unwed mother-hood and illegitimacy has been greatly reduced. As a result, the proportion of babies born to unwed mothers increased from 5.3 percent to 30 percent between 1960 and 1996. This number is even higher among African Americans: sixty-eight percent of African American babies are born to unmarried women. African American single-parent families are concentrated in poverty-stricken inner-city neighborhoods, where rates of violent juvenile crime are highest.

Due to society's increasing tolerance of divorce and unwed motherhood, America has seen a dramatic increase in the number of single-parent families, most of which are headed by mothers rather than fathers. The number of American children living in single-parent families rose from 5.8 million to 18 million between 1960 and 1996.

Welfare's Contribution

The rise in single-parent families, especially among minorities in the inner cities, has been encouraged by the ready availability of welfare. Although the welfare reform law signed by President Bill Clinton in 1996 places new limits on these programs, it will take time to undo the damage done by decades of excessively liberal policies.

There is no doubt that welfare has encouraged illegitimacy. Welfare's guarantee of financial security for unwed mothers has eliminated the economic disincentive to bear children outside of marriage. Robert Rector, a policy analyst at the Heritage Foundation, a conservative think tank, explains how welfare contributes to illegitimacy in the inner cities:

> Largely because of welfare, illegitimacy and single parenthood have become the conventional "lifestyle option" for raising children in many low-income communities. . . . While young women do not necessarily bear unwanted children in order to reap windfall profits from welfare, they are very much aware of the role welfare will play in supporting

them once a child is born. Thus, the availability of welfare plays an important role in influencing a woman's decision to have a child out of wedlock.[2]

The Absence of Fathers

By encouraging out-of-wedlock births, the welfare system effectively eliminates the father from the family. Indeed, welfare recipients risk losing their benefits if they choose to marry. In a sense, then, welfare has replaced the man as the husband and father of the family. Charles Augustus Ballard, the founder and president of the National Institute for Responsible Fatherhood and Family Development, explains how welfare diminishes the role and presence of fathers in inner-city families:

> The vast majority of assistance programs . . . are aimed at young mothers. At best, fathers are irrelevant; invisible men drifting in and out of their children's lives. At worse, fathers are a presence that can disqualify a mother for government benefits. Fathers . . . get the message: They are a problem—an obstacle in the path of a system built to help single mothers cope.
>
> I sometimes wonder whether any of us appreciate the radical experiment we are conducting in the inner cities of America. In all of history we have never seen a stable society without fathers. Yet just a society seems to be the aim of our social policy.[3]

Whether in the inner cities or the suburbs, the lack of a father can have detrimental consequences for a teenager, especially—but certainly not exclusively—a teenage boy. As William J. Bennett, the former U.S. secretary of education and a well-known commentator on America's social and moral issues, states,

> Although single women can do a fine job raising children . . . it is a lot harder to do it alone. . . . You cannot raise young boys to become responsible citizens

unless there are other good men in their lives—men who will spend time with them, discipline them and love them. [4]

The consequences of being without a father can be tragic. While girls without fathers are more likely to become pregnant at an early age, fatherless boys are more apt to join gangs. As Michael Tanner, the director of health and welfare studies for the Cato Institute, a libertarian think tank, writes,

> Boys growing up in mother only families naturally seek male influences. Unfortunately, in many inner city neighborhoods, those male role models do not exist. . . . Thus, the boy in search of male guidance and companionship may end up in the company of gangs or other undesirable influences. [5]

And while in the company of these influences, he is apt to succumb to the temptations of drug use and crime—including violent crime. As Ballard states, the absence of fathers is at the root of the youth violence that plagues the inner cities:

> Look at the social pathologies that plague us today: drug abuse, homicide, gang violence, crime. Now survey the youth who fall prey to any or all of those calamities, and ask them where their father was when their lives took a turn for the worse. Or visit our prisons and ask the men locked up what role their father played in their lives. You'll find too many say, "no role at all." [6]

It is up to all of us to reverse the process of family disintegration that has left teenagers adrift without the discipline and guidance of fathers and other positive male role models. To protect the nation's young people, as well as our own future, we must commit ourselves to mending split families and nurturing new unions so that they remain intact.

1. Barbara Dafoe Whitehead, "Dan Quayle Was Right," *Atlantic Monthly*, April 1993, p. 77.

2. Robert Rector, "Welfare Reform," in *Issues '96: The Candidate's Briefing Book.* Washington, DC: Heritage Foundation, 1996.

3. Charles Augustus Ballard, "Prodigal Dad: How We Bring Fathers Home to Their Children," *Policy Review*, Winter 1995, p. 66.

4. House Ways and Means Committee, William J. Bennett testifying before the Subcommittee on Human Resources, January 20, 1995.

5. Senate Judiciary Committee, Michael Tanner testifying before the Subcommittee on Youth Violence, June 7, 1995.

6. Ballard, "Prodigal Dad," p. 66.

"Those who blame the breakdown of the family for teen violence gloss over the realities of poverty, guns, and discrimination that are the true roots of the problem."

The Breakdown of the Family Is Not the Cause of Teen Violence

It has become fashionable to blame all of society's problems on the breakdown of the traditional two-parent family and the demise of "family values." We have been told repeatedly that children who grow up with only one parent (usually their mother) are vulnerable to a wide range of problems in life, including poverty, emotional disorders, teenage pregnancy—and teen violence.

This focus on the single-parent family structure is misplaced. It is true that the family structure has changed; the number of single-parent families has risen dramatically in recent decades. It is also true that a single-parent family is more likely to be poor than a two-parent family. But it does not follow from these facts that the single-parent family structure is the source of all of society's social problems and the root cause of teen violence.

Correlation Does Not Prove Causation

For argument's sake, let's assume that it is true that teenagers from single-parent homes are more likely to commit violence.

This fact does not prove that the single-parent family structure is the cause of the violent behavior. As psychologists Arlene Skolnick and Stacey Rosencranz state, this type of reasoning "ignores the principle taught in elementary statistics that correlation does not prove causation."[1] Skolnick and Rosencranz point out that the actual cause of the problem might lie in any of a number of factors:

> Single-parenthood may be correlated with many problems affecting children, but the causes may lie elsewhere—for example, in economic and emotional problems affecting parents that lead to difficulties raising children and greater chances of divorce.[2]

Blaming teen violence on single-parent families and women who have babies out of wedlock is a simplistic response to a complex problem.

If the breakdown of the traditional family structure is not to blame for teenage violence, what is? Several factors stand out as key causes: growing up amid poverty and violence, the availability of guns, and discrimination against women and minorities.

The Role of Poverty and Violence

The primary cause of teen violence is poverty. If single-parent families are more likely to raise teens who commit violence, it is because such families are more likely to be poor. Indeed, approximately 50 percent of female-headed families with children under eighteen live in poverty. It is the poverty of these families, rather than their structure, that produces violence.

Mike Males, the author of *The Scapegoat Generation: America's War on Adolescents*, has studied violent crime and has concluded that violence is caused by "the stresses of economic adversity."[3] As proof, he points out that the rates of violence were high during the Great Depression, when the nation suffered perhaps its severest poverty in history. He also compares the crime rates in poor areas with those in more affluent areas.

Examining California, he writes, "Fresno, California's poorest major county, suffers violent crime rates double those of Ventura, one of the state's richest."[4]

The fact that poverty, not the single-parent family structure, is the true cause of teenage violence is borne out by sociological evidence. In a review of the sociological literature on the subject, Kevin N. Wright, a professor of criminal justice, and Karen E. Wright, who works for the Planned Parenthood Association, conclude that "economic conditions inherent to single-parent families may place children at greater risk"[5] of delinquency. Findings such as this suggest that rather than lamenting the decline of two-parent families, society should focus on providing single-parent families with the economic resources they need to raise children successfully.

Along with poverty, the presence of violence in the home and community contributes to the problem of teen violence. According to Delbert S. Elliott, the director of the Center for the Study and Prevention of Violence at the University of Boulder, children exposed to violence and physical abuse in the home face a 40 percent increased risk of engaging in violence as teenagers. In addition to violence in the home, the quality of the neighborhood can also impact a teenager's involvement with violence. Young people who live in poor, violent neighborhoods with an abundance of drugs and gang activity are more likely to become involved in violent behavior—including gang violence.

The Availability of Guns

Guns are a major contributor to the problem of teen violence. There are 200 million guns circulating in American society—60 to 70 million of which are handguns. These guns often find their way into the hands of young people and are frequently used in violent crimes—including the murder of teenagers. According to a report published by the Office of Juvenile Justice and Delinquency Prevention (OJJDP), the number of juveniles killed by firearms nearly tripled between 1984 and

.ı-related murders are the leading cause of death for .ı American teenagers between the ages of fifteen and .eteen. The Educational Fund to End Handgun Violence reports that guns are responsible for 60 percent of deaths among black males ages fifteen to nineteen and 23 percent of whites in the same age group. These statistics suggest that the large number of guns in the possession of the nation's young people should be a major cause of concern.

There are several reasons why guns are so dangerous in the hands of teenagers. First, teenagers are still too young to have complete control over their emotions and impulses. Second, they are less able to completely grasp the possible tragic results of pulling the trigger. James Alan Fox, the dean of the College of Criminal Justice at Northeastern University, explains why a teenager with a gun is such a threat:

> A 14-year-old armed with a gun is far more menac-
> ing than a 44-year-old with a gun. Although juveniles
> may be untrained in using firearms, they are more

The easy availabilty of handguns and the impulsiveness of teens can make a deadly combination.

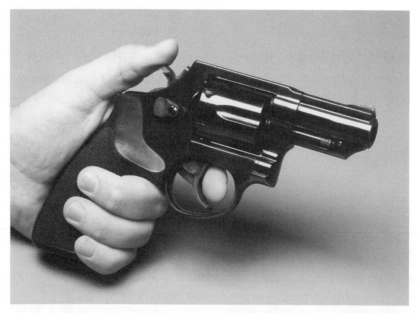

willing to pull the trigger over trivial matters—a leather jacket, a pair of sneakers, a challenging remark, or no reason at all—without fully considering the consequences.[6]

Gender and Racial Discrimination

Gender discrimination also contributes to the problem of teenage violence. As noted earlier, about 50 percent of female-headed single-parent families are poor. This poverty has its roots in women's inequality in American society. As of 1992, women who worked full-time earned approximately 70 percent of the wages earned by full-time male workers. In addition, women face significant barriers to advancement in the American labor market. According to Barbara F. Reskin and Irene Padavic, "Women are concentrated at low levels in the organizations that employ them and in the lower ranks in their occupations and professions."[7] Thus, due to gender discrimination inherent in the U.S. economic system, children of mother-headed families face a significant risk of poverty. The violence that results from this poverty should be blamed on the inequality that impedes women's economic progress, not on the single mother.

Racial discrimination also plays a role in teenage violence. The OJJDP has reported that minority juveniles are arrested at rates disproportionately higher than whites. This disparity exists not because minorities are inherently violent but because they are more likely to be poor. Minority single mothers suffer under the double burden of gender discrimination and racial discrimination. Their children, in turn, are impeded due to racial discrimination that limits their educational, job training, and employment opportunities as they attempt to make the transition to adulthood. As Elliott states, in minority neighborhoods, "conventional opportunities are limited by racism, discrimination, social isolation from the labor market, and few resources."[8] Faced with these circumstances, adolescents—especially adolescent males—often lash

...ntly in anger or frustration. They also become disillusioned in their search for legitimate employment and after-school activities and turn to crime and gang involvement.

Those who blame the breakdown of the family for teen violence gloss over the realities of poverty, guns, and discrimination that are the true roots of the problem. Rather than stigmatizing single mothers, society should mobilize its resources to ensure that the children of this country receive the support they need to mature into thoughtful, civilized, and compassionate adults.

1. Arlene Skolnick and Stacey Rosencranz, "The New Crusade for the Old Family," *American Prospect*, Summer 1994, p. 61.

2. Skolnick and Rosencranz, "The New Crusade for the Old Family," p. 61.

3. Michael A. Males, "Executioner's Myth," *Los Angeles Times*, May 4, 1997, p. M1.

4. Males, "Executioner's Myth," p. M1.

5. Kevin N. Wright and Karen E. Wright, *Family Life, Delinquency, and Crime: A Policymaker's Guide*. Washington, DC: Office of Juvenile Justice and Delinquency Prevention, May 1994.

6. James Alan Fox, "Should the Federal Government Have a Major Role in Reducing Juvenile Crime? Pro," *Congressional Digest*, August/September 1996, p. 208.

7. Barbara F. Reskin and Irene Padavic, *Women and Men at Work*. Thousand Oaks, CA: Pine Forge Press, 1994.

8. Delbert S. Elliott, "Youth Violence: An Overview," working paper, Center for the Study of Youth Policy, University of Pennsylvania, Philadelphia, 1993.

"Media violence teaches teens to be aggressive, inures them to the consequences of their violent acts, and causes them to view the world as a dangerously violent place."

Media Violence Causes Teen Violence

On March 24, 1998, thirteen-year-old Mitchell Johnson and his eleven-year-old accomplice, Andrew Golden, opened fire on a schoolyard in Jonesboro, Arkansas, killing four students and one teacher and wounding several others. In the aftermath of the shooting, Arkansas governor Mike Huckabee said in dismay, "I don't know what else we'd expect in a culture where children are exposed to tens of thousands of murders on television and movies. We've desensitized human life."[1]

According to the American Medical Association, the average American child witnesses two hundred thousand acts of violence on television—including sixteen thousand murders— by the age of eighteen. In addition, children and teenagers play violent video games for hours on end, listen to music with violent lyrics, and thrill to the violent fare produced by the Hollywood movie industry. For over twenty years, social scientists and government experts have been stating definitively that exposure to all this violence contributes to violent behavior among teens.

Some people deny that media violence causes teen violence. They claim that the studies prove a *correlation* between media violence and teen violence, but not that media violence *causes* teen violence. These doubters ignore the mounds of scientific evidence that have been collected over the years. As the American Academy of Pediatrics states, "American media are the most violent in the world, and American society is now paying a high price in terms of real-life violence."[2]

Studies on Television Violence

Over one thousand studies have proven the connection between television violence and real-life violence. In laboratory studies dating back to the 1950s, researchers have observed how children react to violent television programs. Children who see violent shows are consistently more likely to engage in aggressive behavior—including hitting and kicking their peers—than those who view nonviolent programs.

In a 1981 epidemiological study, Brandon Centerwall concluded that television was the cause of the dramatic increase in U.S. murder rates in the mid-1950s. By that time, he argued, television had been an integral part of society long enough for its violence-causing effects to become apparent. To prove his theory, Centerwall compared the U.S. murder rates to those of South Africa, where television was banned until 1975. He found that the murder rates in South Africa rose sharply approximately twelve years after the introduction of television. He concluded that the similarities in the murder rates following the introduction of television in the two countries, occurring three decades apart, proved that television causes violent behavior.

Between 1960 and 1982 Leonard Eron of the University of Illinois and Rowell Huesmann of the University of Michigan studied the connection between violent television and aggressive behavior in children, teenagers, and adults. They established that exposure to television violence not only causes aggressiveness among young children, but that it also causes violent behavior later in life. First they studied eight-year-olds and found that those who watched the most violent television were the most aggressive. Then they studied the same subjects

at ages nineteen and thirty and discovered that th
watched the most television violence as eight-year-ʋ..
more likely to be violent as teens and adults.

These and other studies have established a clear cause-and-effect relationship between television violence and violent behavior. This connection has been confirmed by government officials and institutions, including the surgeon general in 1972 and the National Institute of Mental Health (NIMH) in 1982. The NIMH stated the issue plainly: "Violent programs on television lead to aggressive behavior by children and teenagers who watch those programs."[3]

Numerous medical professional organizations concur, including the American Psychological Association and the American Academy of Pediatrics (AAP). According to the AAP, "The vast majority of studies conclude that there is a cause-and-effect relationship between media violence and real-life violence. This link is undeniable and uncontestable."[4]

Video Games and the Internet

Although most studies have focused on violence on television, their findings apply to other media as well. For example, violent video and Internet games, which occupy a significant portion of many teenagers' days, are clearly a risk. According to Mediascope, a nonprofit media education organization,

> While studies on video games and aggressive behavior must be considered preliminary, it may be reasonably inferred from more than 1,000 reports and studies on television violence that video game violence may also contribute to aggressive behavior and desensitization to violence.[5]

Moreover, with video games and the Internet, young people are transformed from passive observers to active participants in the violence. The added element of interaction takes teens one step closer to committing the real act. As explained by Brian Stonehill, the founder of the media studies program

...ona College in Claremont, California, "The technology is going from passive to active. . . . The violence is no longer vicarious with interactive media. It's much more pernicious and worrisome."[6]

Gangsta Rap

Rap music is another form of media that contributes to the problem of teen violence. While not all rap music promotes violence, the style known as "gangsta rap" contains lyrics that celebrate and blatantly encourage aggressiveness. It is clear that this so-called art form has real-world consequences. Nathan McCall, the author of *Makes Me Wanna Holler: A Young Black Man in America*, explains how rap music and lyrics fuel youth violence:

> It may be crazy to tie music to behavior. But the history of African-Americans shows that, from the days of slavery to the present, music has always been an agent of change. And rap is more than rhyming words. It's the central part of a powerful cultural movement—hip-hop—that influences the way young blacks walk, talk, dress and think.
>
> The key element is aggression—in the rappers' body language, tone and witty rhymes—that often leaves listeners hyped, on edge, angry.[7]

The lyrics not only promote violence between males but also by males against females. In gangsta rap, according to McCall, "women are 'bitches and hos,' disposable playthings who exist merely for men's abusive delight."[8]

In addition to performing violently provocative music and lyrics, rappers encourage violence by serving as inappropriate role models for young blacks. As McCall states,

> Young blacks look to rappers . . . as people they want to emulate. And because they feel powerless, these youths are consumed with the symbols of power—guns and gangstas.

> They imagine themselves Godfathers and, sadly, some actually get up the nerve to act out such roles.[9]

The influence of gangsta rap helps to explain why youth violence disproportionately affects African American communities—and why gun violence is the leading cause of death among black teenagers.

How Media Violence Causes Violence

Media violence causes real-life teen violence by modeling and legitimizing aggressive behavior. However, it promotes violence in other ways as well. The *National Television Violence Study* (*NTVS*), an analysis of television content begun in 1994 by Mediascope and a group of four universities, found that in television programs, perpetrators of violence frequently go unpunished and violence often involves no harm or pain to the victims. Thus, television teaches teens that violence is an effective and harmless way to solve problems and get what they want.

Because violence is portrayed as having few consequences for perpetrators or victims, the *NTVS* concludes that television

violence poses three risks to viewers: "The risk of viewing the most common depictions of televised violence include learning to behave violently, becoming more desensitized to the harmful consequences of violence, and becoming more fearful of being attacked."[10] While this conclusion refers to the effects of televised mayhem, it applies equally to all forms of media violence. In sum, media violence teaches teens to be aggressive, inures them to the consequences of their violent acts, and causes them to view the world as a dangerously violent place—a phenomenon commonly referred to as the "mean world" effect. Clearly, teens who view the world as a mean place are more likely to accept violence as a commonplace occurrence and to engage in violence themselves.

A Disservice

The harmful effects of media violence have been verified by numerous studies and by major medical professional organizations. Those who deny this reality and claim that the correlation between media violence and real-life violence is meaningless are doing a grave disservice to the country's youths.

1. Quoted in Sandy Grady, "The Questions After Jonesboro," *San Diego Union-Tribune*, March 27, 1998, p. B-10.

2. American Academy of Pediatrics, "Media Violence," *Pediatrics*, June 1995.

3. Quoted in "Violence on Television: What Do Children Learn? What Can Parents Do?" American Psychological Association, 1998. On-line. Internet. Available http://www.apa. org/pubinfo/violence.html.

4. Quoted in American Academy of Pediatrics, "Media Violence."

5. Mediascope, "Video Game Violence," issue brief, n.d. On-line. Internet. Available http://www.igc.apc.org/mediascope/fvidviol.htm.

6. Quoted in Gloria Goodale, "Battles over Media Violence Move to a New Frontier: The Internet," *Christian Science Monitor*, November 18, 1996, p. 10.

7. Nathan McCall, "My Rap Against Rap," *Washington Post*, November 14, 1993.

8. McCall, "My Rap Against Rap."

9. McCall, "My Rap Against Rap."

10. "Summary of Findings and Recommendations," *National Television Violence Study, 1994–1995*. On-line. Internet. Available http://www.mediascope.org/medias.

"Studies do not prove that watching violent programs causes teens to commit violent acts."

Media Violence Does Not Cause Teen Violence

Critics of media violence like to claim that over one thousand studies have proven that viewing television violence causes violent behavior (some even say that three thousand such studies have been done). Based on these studies, sociologists and public health officials declare that media violence in general—including violence on television programs, motion pictures, video games, and rock and rap music—entices teenagers to commit violent acts. Even if it were scientifically valid to apply the findings of television violence studies to other media, these critics would still be wrong. In fact, fewer than one hundred studies have focused specifically on the causal link between television violence and real-life aggression. Moreover, contrary to the claims of alarmists, these studies do not prove that watching violent programs causes teens to commit violent acts.

Laboratory Studies

Many of the studies on television violence have been done in laboratories. Typically, one group of children is shown a violent program and another is shown a nonviolent program. Then both groups are tested on their aggressiveness. Some studies have found that the children who see violent programs are more likely to behave aggressively afterwards than those who view nonviolent programs.

While these studies seem convincing on the surface, they are problematic for several reasons. First, because they take place in laboratories, their results cannot be generalized to the real world. Second, it is impossible to determine whether the aggressive behavior observed is a reaction to the violent television show or an attempt on the part of the child to meet the adult researchers' expectations. As Kevin Durkin, an associate professor of psychology at the University of Western Australia, states, "Even quite young children are good at working out what adults want them to do, or will let them get away with."[1] Finally, the aggressive behavior seen in these studies is a short-term response to stimuli; it does not indicate that the child is on the path to becoming a violent career criminal.

Correlational Studies

In addition to laboratory studies, correlational studies have been done to determine whether the two variables (television violence and real-life violence) are related. Rather than taking place in the laboratory, these studies collect information on young people's viewing habits and on their behavior. The most widely cited correlational study was conducted by Leonard Eron of the University of Illinois and Rowell Huesmann of the University of Michigan. Beginning in 1960, they studied a group of eight-year-old boys and found a correlation between watching violent television shows and behaving aggressively. Eleven years later, the boys who had watched the most violent television at age eight were the most violent at age nineteen.

The main problem with correlational studies is that even though a correlation may exist between children's watching violent television shows and behaving aggressively, this does not prove that the violent television programs *cause* the violent behavior. It could just as reasonably be argued that viewing violent television programs is caused by the child's preexisting tendency to be aggressive. Jonathan Freedman, a professor of psychology at the University of Toronto, explains the problem of assuming that a correlation implies causation:

> Correlations do not prove causality. Boys watch more TV football than girls, and they play more football than girls, but no one, so far as I know, believes that television is what makes boys more interested in football. Probably personality characteristics that make children more aggressive also make them prefer violent television programs.[2]

In addition, the correlation between viewing violent television shows and behaving violently may be caused by a third variable, such as poor parenting. As Durkin explains, "High television is correlated with lax parenting; aggressive behaviour in children is also correlated with lax parenting; hence, it is possible that the real source of the problem is family management."[3]

The argument that media violence causes real-life teen violence hinges primarily on overzealous claims about study findings. Those who say this or that study proves a link between television violence and aggressive behavior ignore the limitations of those studies. Durkin succinctly sums up the state of the research:

> Each of the principal means of investigation of the effects of violent television content has its drawbacks and, quite properly, research into such a complex topic will inevitably be open to criticism. However, even if we accept the findings of the most prominent research, such as Eron and Huesmann's, they tell us that the relationship between viewing and aggressive behaviour is a weak one. Nobody has ever demonstrated otherwise.[4]

Gangsta Rap

Those who blame teen violence on the media are fond of targeting rap music—especially "gangsta rap"—for special criticism. The violent deaths of two major rap stars (Tupac Shakur

The violent gangsta rap lyrics of such artists as Tupac Shakur (pictured) are blamed for influencing teens to commit violent acts.

and the Notorious B.I.G.) in the mid-1990s seemed to confirm that gangsta rap breeds violence.

Gangsta rap does often contain graphically violent lyrics that are delivered in an aggressive style. And it is obvious that many teenage boys, including whites, admire and emulate rap stars, assuming their aggressive postures, attitudes, and speech patterns. However, it is a huge leap of logic to conclude that just because these teens adopt an aggressive demeanor they believe that violent behavior is acceptable or that they are more inclined to commit violent acts. The vast majority of teens make the correct moral distinction between acting tough and committing violent crimes.

Rather than promoting violence, rap reflects the reality of life in the inner cities, which are plagued by unemployment, poverty, racial discrimination, and black-on-black violence. While the music may be disturbing, it points to a disturbing reality. Tricia Rose, an assistant professor at New York University, explains how rap music chronicles life in the inner cities:

Many rappers are able to codify the everyday experiences of demonized young black men and bear witness to the experiences they face, never see explained from their perspective, but know are true. Many a gangsta rap tale chronicles the experience of wandering around all day, trying to make order out of a horizon of unemployment, gang cultural occupation, the threat of violence from police and rival teens, and fragile home relationships. [5]

Instead of focusing blame on rap music, society should address the deplorable social conditions described in the music. As syndicated columnist Clarence Page writes, "It is not enough for us parents to denounce rap CDs and tapes and snatch them out of children's hands. . . . Rather we have to give kids something to believe in." [6]

Irresponsible Leadership

To state that media violence has not been proven to cause real-life violence is not to defend media violence on artistic or aesthetic grounds. Television programs, Hollywood films, rock and rap music, and other media do contain too much gratuitous violence. Young people would be better off reading a good book than tuning in to the latest Hollywood action adventure film or the newest gangsta rap CD. However, blaming media violence as the cause of real-world violence among teenagers is irresponsible.

The nation's leaders have chosen to blame media violence because it is easy. By criticizing the media for airing too much violence, they give the impression that they are doing something about the violence that pervades American society. In the process, they also deflect the public's attention from the real—and more difficult—causes of teen violence: poverty, unemployment, racial discrimination, easy access to guns, and a lack of legitimate educational and employment opportunities for inner-city youth. As Todd Gitlin, a professor of sociology at the University of California at Berkeley, states,

The attempt to demonize the media distracts attention from the real causes of—and the serious remedies for—the epidemic of violence. . . . Violence on the screens, however loathsome, does not make a significant contribution to violence on the streets. Images don't spill blood. Rage, equipped with guns, does. Desperation does. Revenge does. As liberals say, the drug trade does; poverty does; unemployment does.[7]

To prevent violence among teenagers, America's leaders must stop blaming fictional threats on TV, video, and movie screens and start addressing the real social problems that confront the nation's young people.

1. Kevin Durkin, "Chasing the Effects of Media Violence," *ABA Update: Newsletter of the Australian Broadcasting Authority*, March 1995. On-line. Internet. Available http://www.screen.com/mnet/eng/issues/violence/resource/articles/chasefx.htm.

2. Jonathan Freedman, "Violence in the Mass Media and Violence in Society: The Link Is Unproven," *Harvard Mental Health Letter*, May 1996.

3. Durkin, "Chasing the Effects of Media Violence."

4. Durkin, "Chasing the Effects of Media Violence."

5. Tricia Rose, "Rap Music and the Demonization of Young Black Males," *USA Today*, May 1994, p. 36.

6. Clarence Page, "B.I.G. Problems at the Root of Rap Violence," *Liberal Opinion Week*, March 24, 1997, p. 5.

7. Todd Gitlin, "Imagebusters," *American Prospect*, Winter 1994, pp. 42, 45.

CHAPTER 3

How Can Teen Violence Be Reduced?

"The young have learned an ominous lesson: They can get away with breaking the law indefinitely with hardly a risk of swift, sure and stern punishment."

Punishment Is the Solution to Teen Violence

Many people believe that when teenagers commit violent crimes they are merely expressing their need for attention. According to this theory, their criminal behavior is a cry for help, a signal for society to step in and provide them with nurturing, social services, and gentle guidance toward the straight-and-narrow path.

The juvenile justice system is founded on the belief that juvenile criminals need help rather than discipline. In fact, the system was established in 1899 precisely because social reformers believed that the criminal justice system was too punitive for juveniles. These advocates thought that because children and teens are still in the process of developing, they can be molded—through guidance, nurturing, and support—into responsible citizens.

Due to the influence of this faith in teens' reformative potential, most teenagers who break the law escape punishment. Often they are simply released into the custody of their parents or guardians, forced to undergo counseling, or subjected to light alternative sentences such as home supervision. When they are incarcerated, they are usually detained for short periods of time, most often in juvenile facilities that emphasize rehabilitation—such as counseling, group therapy, vocational training, and other services—rather than punishment.

In addition, because the privacy of juvenile delinquents is protected, their identities are not made public, shielding them from the censure of their communities. Moreover, their prior misdeeds cannot be used as evidence against them in court. Consequently, often their second, third, or fourth offense draws a sentence as light as their first crime.

A Revolving Door

Because the juvenile justice system treats teens with excessive leniency—in the form of light sentences, rehabilitative services rather than harsh punishment, and numerous "second chances"—it has created a "revolving door" that returns teens to the streets again and again, enabling them to commit one violent act after another. As Woody West, the associate editor of *Insight* magazine, states,

> As a result of what has become a congenitally feeble juvenile criminal-justice system—to the extent that not even names, as a rule, can be made public in heinous crimes—the young have learned an ominous lesson: They can get away with breaking the law indefinitely with hardly a risk of swift, sure and stern punishment.[1]

This inadequate response to violence leaves society vulnerable to the exploits of violence-prone teens. And it is not just adults who are at risk of victimization. The nation's young are at greatest risk. As John J. DiIulio Jr., a scholar at the Brookings Institution, a public-policy think tank, concludes, "Unless we close the revolving door on juvenile crime, we will close the coffin on more juveniles."[2]

Time to Get Tough

Rather than pretending that teens who commit violent crime are simply children who have gone astray, society needs to acknowledge that many of them are hard-core criminals who feel no remorse for their crimes. A study conducted in Philadelphia in 1972 found that 6 percent of the juvenile population was responsible for two-thirds of the violent juvenile crime in that city. This 6 percent of chronic offenders (those who have five or more contacts with the police) are youths who have demonstrated through their actions that they are incapable of refraining from criminal activity. When allowed to roam free, they present an unacceptable risk to society. Therefore, such teens should be captured and incarcerated in secure detention facilities for long periods of time. James Wootten and Robert O. Heck, authors of the article "How State and Local Officials Can Combat Violent Juvenile Crime," write:

> In many states, the greatest single weakness of the effort to combat juvenile crime is a simple failure to target the most dangerous young offenders. This weakness arises from a reluctance on the part of juvenile justice officials to admit that there is a point at which a delinquent youth becomes such a threat to the community that he or she must be held accountable and incarcerated. [3]

The Office of Juvenile Justice and Delinquency Prevention (OJJDP), the section of the U.S. Department of Justice that focuses on juvenile crime, acknowledges the need to lock up a significant proportion of violent teens. According to the OJJDP, "The criminal behavior of many serious, violent, and chronic juvenile offenders requires the application of secure sanctions to hold these offenders accountable for their delinquent acts." [4]

However, the OJJDP does not go far enough. While conceding that incarceration is necessary in extreme cases, the

OJJDP clings to the doctrine of rehabilitation and treatment for even the most hardened juvenile criminals. To adequately protect society and deter teens from committing violent crime, the OJJDP and other juvenile justice institutions must give up their fantasy that all violent juveniles can be reformed. As DiIulio clearly states, these institutions must accept the need to incarcerate increasing numbers of violent youths:

> No one relishes the thought of locking up more juveniles. But it must be done. The federal Office of Juvenile Justice and Delinquency Prevention (OJJDP) should be directed to assist the states in securely, humanly, and cost-effectively incarcerating kids who criminally violate the life, liberty, and property of others. OJJDP and the rest of the federal juvenile justice establishment needs to get out of its anti-incarceration time warp.[5]

Public Safety and Deterrence

There are at least two reasons why society should take a more punitive stance toward juvenile crime. The first and most important is public safety. By targeting the worst violators and locking them up, society can reduce the odds that law-abiding citizens—including the 94 percent of juveniles who are not chronic offenders—will be victimized by teen criminals.

Second, subjecting violent teens to lengthy jail terms will have a deterrent effect. It will send a signal to other teens that violent behavior will result in severe repercussions, including the loss of liberty for much of their adult life. This message will encourage teens to avoid the temptation to engage in violent criminal acts.

Changing the System

Various policy changes would enable society to provide violent teenage criminals with the punishment they deserve. First, more violent juveniles should be tried in criminal (adult) courts rather than in the juvenile courts. In adult courts, juveniles are subjected to adult time in adult institutions rather than the relatively mild sentences imposed by the juvenile system.

If a teen does remain in the juvenile system, the judge should be allowed to take that teen's past crimes into account at the time of sentencing. This would free judges to impose harsher sentences. Moreover, the identities of violent teens in the juvenile system should be made public. This disclosure would allow communities to protect themselves from violent juveniles who are released back into their midst. It would also expose violent juvenile criminals to the reformative power of public shaming.

Three Strikes

In addition to trying more juveniles as adults and eliminating the privacy that protects teens from appropriate scrutiny, "three strikes" legislation should be included in the fight against violent juvenile crime. Three strikes laws, which already apply to adults in many states, mandate that criminals convicted of their third serious felony receive a lengthy prison sentence. This policy should be extended to apply to juveniles. In explaining his rationale for a juvenile three strikes bill proposed in California, Assembly Speaker Cruz M. Bustamante, states:

> Incredibly, a juvenile can now commit three, four, five or even more felonies . . . and face punishment no more severe than home supervision. If kids get the message they can repeatedly commit crimes and not do time, the credibility of the entire system is in danger.[6]

Three strikes laws and other reforms of the justice system are clearly necessary to send a clear message to would-be violent teens: No longer will your disregard for the rights of your fellow citizens be tolerated and indulged. No longer will you be given free reign to commit repeated acts of violence.

No longer will your crimes be met with efforts to nurture, heal, and reform you. Instead, you will be punished in a manner proportionate to the severity of your crime.

1. Woody West, "A Slap on the Wrist for 'Naughty' Kids," *Insight*, August 19, 1996, p. 48.

2. Senate, John J. DiIulio Jr. speaking before the Subcommittee on Youth Violence, February 28, 1996.

3. James Wootton and Robert O. Heck, "How State and Local Officials Can Combat Violent Juvenile Crime," *Heritage Foundation Backgrounder*, October 28, 1996.

4. Office of Juvenile Justice and Delinquency Prevention, *Comprehensive Strategy for Serious, Violent, and Chronic Juvenile Offenders: Program Summary*. Washington, DC: Office of Juvenile Justice and Delinquency Prevention, 1994, p. 21.

5. Senate, DiIulio.

6. Quoted in "Speaker's Three Strikes for Juveniles, Boot Camp Bills Move Forward," press release, April 22, 1997. On-line. Internet. Available http://www.assembly.ca.gov/demweb/members/a31/press/p3197019.htm.

"The real challenge for our nation is not how many jails we can build, but how many kids we can save."

Prevention Is the Solution to Teen Violence

Many politicians and law enforcement officials argue that the best solution to the problem of teen violence is to crack down on violent teenage criminals. They advocate changing the laws to make it easier to try and sentence juveniles as adults. They also call for building more prisons in which to incarcerate violent teens for longer periods of time. This tactic, proponents believe, will protect society from violent youths and send the message to would-be teen criminals that violence will not be condoned.

Those who support this punitive approach have their priorities backward. Rather than coming down hard on teens who commit violent acts, adult society should be trying to stop the violence that seems to have become so pervasive in America. As concisely stated by Teresa Nelson, the executive director of the American Civil Liberties Union of Georgia, "The real challenge for our nation is not how many jails we can build, but how many kids we can save."[1]

The punitive response to juvenile crime is flawed for several reasons. First, it is fatalistic; it assumes that society is powerless to help adolescents overcome the problems that lead to trouble with the law. Second, it sends teens the message that society does not care enough to try to help them. Third, it fails to address the underlying causes of teen violence, including poverty, a lack of positive adult role models, inadequate employment opportunities, and other social problems. Finally, it is reactive rather than proactive; it attempts to solve the problem after it has occurred rather than heading it off in the first place.

Prevention Is the Solution

The answer to the juvenile violence problem is not to wait for such violence to occur and then lock up the perpetrator and throw away the key. The solution is to prevent such violence from taking place at all.

One important aspect of violence prevention is early involvement. Because children who are abused and neglected have an increased risk of committing violence as teens, home visitation programs should be used to monitor children who are at risk of abuse or neglect, and the parents of such children should be provided with education to enhance their parenting skills. According to Shay Bilchik, the administrator of the Office of Juvenile Justice and Delinquency Prevention (OJJDP), this measure would "build the foundation for law-abiding lives for children and interrupt the cycle of violence that can turn abused or neglected children into delinquents."[2]

Another aspect of prevention involves intervening at the first sign of trouble instead of waiting until a more serious problem has occurred. As Bilchik puts it,

> Kids . . . give off warning signs—running away, skipping school, failing academically, acting out aggressively or showing signs of abuse or neglect. An effective violence-reduction strategy does not ignore these early symptoms but rather treats them directly . . . putting the broken pieces of children's lives back together again.[3]

As Bilchik suggests, by identifying teens who are at risk of trouble, society can head off the violence that too often ruins—or ends—young people's lives.

Community-Based Programs and Mentoring

In addition to intervening early, society needs to provide older teens with legitimate activities during the after-school hours. Many successful community-based programs have been developed across the country through both government and grassroots efforts. These programs offer young people a safe haven from street violence or chaotic home lives, a place to play sports and develop their artistic talents, and the company of positive adult role models and supportive peers.

The Northeast Performing Arts (NEPA) organization in Washington, D.C., serves as an example of the positive contribution that grassroots community-based organizations can make to the nation's young people. Public housing resident Rita Jackson founded the organization in 1979 in one of the poorest regions of the city. Originally designed as a safe house that provided drama and dance classes, NEPA has grown to include programs that offer mentoring, career counseling, assistance in starting a business, and academic guidance. According to Robert L. Woodson, the president of the National Center for Neighborhood Enterprise in Washington, D.C., NEPA has served more than twelve hundred youths, many of whom have gone on to college and to successful performing arts careers. Woodson attributes the organization's success to Jackson's leadership:

> Rita Jackson's consistent, unconditional support has nurtured a sense of hope, confidence, and self-worth in the hearts of young people who had been told throughout their lives that there is no reason to hope. That support has made all the difference.[4]

Many other organizations, including the Boys and Girls Clubs nationwide, provide a similar function, guiding teens away from violence and toward success.

As Rita Jackson's example shows, to prevent violent juvenile crime, adults must become involved in young people's lives. This fact is demonstrated by the success of the nation's largest mentoring program, Big Brothers/Big Sisters (BB/BS) of America. In BB/BS, adult volunteers provide youths from single-parent families with companionship, support, and guidance. A study comparing the behavior of BB/BS participants to non-participants reveals that the presence of a genuinely concerned adult can make a crucial difference in a teenager's life. The study found that participants were significantly less likely to engage in a variety of antisocial behaviors—including violence. Mentored youths were one-third less likely than nonmentored youths to hit another person.

Prevention Is More Effective

Other studies lend additional support to the view that prevention is more effective than punishment. RAND, a public policy research institution, compared four prevention programs similar to those described earlier to the "three strikes" program, which mandates incarceration after a juvenile's third offense. RAND concluded that three of the prevention approaches were more cost-effective than imprisonment: parent training, offering cash and other incentives to high school students to graduate, and supervision of juveniles who have committed previous delinquent behavior. According to RAND, spending $1 million on graduation incentives can prevent more than 250 crimes per year, while spending the same amount on imprisonment can prevent only 60 crimes per year.

The RAND study brings home the fact that prevention programs are a better solution to the problem of teen violence than punishment. Rather than constructing more prisons, passing "three strikes" laws, and trying juveniles as adults, society should instead invest in programs designed to provide teens with support, opportunities, and guidance. It may be easier to simply wait until a teenager has committed a violent crime and then apply a predetermined punishment, but by taking this approach, adults fail in their responsibility to care enough for young people to get involved in their lives and help them avoid the temptations that lead to violence. As stated by the Children's Defense Fund, an organization that promotes policies to help children, "The opportunity is ripe to increase investments in proven prevention strategies for teenagers and young children, so they can become nonviolent youths who achieve success in their families, schools, friendships, and activities."[5]

1. Teresa Nelson, ACLU press release, April 10, 1996. On-line. Internet. Available http://www.aclu.org/news.n041096.html.

2. Shay Bilchik, "Saving America's Children—a Little at the Time," *San Diego Union-Tribune*, September 18, 1997, p. B-9.

3. Bilchik, "Saving America's Children—a Little at the Time," p. B-9.

4. Robert L. Woodson, "Reclaiming the Lives of Young People," *USA Today*, September 1997.

5. Children's Defense Fund, *The State of America's Children: Yearbook 1997*. Washington, DC: Children's Defense Fund, 1997, p. 63.

"For those teens who persist in committing adult crimes, society should mete out adult punishments."

Violent Teens Should Be Tried and Sentenced as Adults

The American ideal of justice holds that a punishment should fit the crime. If someone commits a relatively minor crime, that person deserves a relatively light sentence. If a person commits an act of brutal violence, that individual deserves to be punished harshly. A system that adheres to this philosophy is the fairest possible.

Unfortunately, the American system does not conform to its own ideal. One class of citizens is allowed to commit violent crimes—including rape, assault, and murder—and receive only a slap on the wrist. The only reason they are treated with such undue leniency is their youthfulness; because they are below the age of legal adulthood, they fall under the purview of the juvenile justice system, which treats lawbreakers much more gingerly than the criminal (adult) system.

This double standard must end. A seventeen-year-old who commits a murder should be treated the same as a nineteen-year-old who commits the exact same crime. Both should be subjected to the same standard of justice; both should get the punishment that fits the crime. In short, both should be tried and sentenced as adults. To let the seventeen-year-old off the hook simply because of age does a disservice to the victim, to society as a whole, and to the ideal of justice. This is the view expressed by syndicated columnist Suzanne Fields when she writes, "We used to say that if a boy is old enough to go to war, he's old enough to drink. If a boy is old enough to rape, he's old enough to do a man's time."[1] The same holds true for murder, assault, and other violent crimes.

The Failure of the Juvenile Justice System

The juvenile justice system deserves a large share of the blame for the problem of violent juvenile crime. The main problem with the system is that it is based on a faulty premise. When first established in 1899, the system's guiding philosophy was that if wayward juveniles received rehabilitation and treatment from professionals, rather than the harsh punishment meted out by the criminal justice system, they could be cured of their propensity for criminal behavior. This belief continues to undergird the system today.

This noble effort may have proven effective in dealing with truants and vandals of an earlier era, but it is entirely inadequate when it comes to today's violent juvenile rapists and murderers. Today's teens not only commit more abhorrent crimes than they did in the past, they show little empathy for their victims, scant remorse for their actions, and no fear of repercussions from the juvenile justice system. Consider the following examples:

Two teenage boys and a young woman repeatedly rape and torture a thirteen-year-old girl, then hang her up in a closet by her feet.

A teenager shoots and paralyzes a jogger who refuses to give him a gold necklace. When asked what could have prevented the attack, the teen says, "He could have given me his rope [chain]. I asked him twice."[2]

Four teenagers rob a Pennsylvania market. One of them shoots the shopkeeper in the head. When two of the teens are arrested, one of them sticks out his tongue at reporters and another makes an obscene gesture.

It is obvious that teens such as these are beyond rehabilitation. They have no respect for life or the rights of others. They either cannot distinguish the difference between right and wrong, or they can distinguish the difference and choose to act in depraved ways. To give such youths rehabilitative treatment is absurd. They should be permanently removed from society.

Expungement

One particular policy of the juvenile justice system is especially problematic. In most states, a juvenile's arrest and conviction records are expunged—that is, sealed or destroyed—when he or she reaches a certain age, usually eighteen. This practice is based on the idea that youthful offenders should be allowed to enter adulthood with a clean slate.

While expungement may be appropriate for a one-time nonviolent offender, it is not appropriate for violent repeat offenders. In effect, it allows violent young criminals to be treated as first-time offenders in court even if they have committed a string of violent crimes. As T. Markus Funk, a clerk for a federal judge in St. Louis, states, "The practice prevents society from acting on the simple fact that those who have committed crimes in the past are likely to commit crimes in the future and hence should be treated differently from true first-time offenders."[3] In this way, the expungement policy assists the careers of violent juvenile criminals by ensuring that they will receive a light sentence and be back on the streets quickly, enabling them to inflict more violence upon society.

The lax treatment meted out by the juvenile system, as exemplified by the expungement policy, sends the message to teens that they will not be held fully accountable for their actions. Therefore, the system fails to provide a disincentive to teens to commit violent crime. The system essentially gives youths a green light to rape, murder, and assault their fellow citizens. Only the adult justice system gives prosecutors and judges the sentencing options that will adequately protect society from violent youths and send the message to would-be violent teens that such behavior will not be tolerated.

Treating Juveniles as Adults

In every state and the District of Columbia, juveniles as young as twelve can be transferred to criminal courts. The number of cases transferred to adult courts has risen dramatically in recent years. According to the Office of Juvenile Justice and Delinquency Prevention (OJJDP), the number of juvenile cases transferred to adult courts increased 71 percent between 1985 and 1994. Support for trying juveniles as adults is not limited to tough-on-crime politicians and law enforcement officials. The movement has wide popular support. In a 1994 *Los Angeles Times* poll, 68 percent of respondents favored treating juveniles who commit violent crimes the same as adults. In a 1994 Gallup poll, 83 percent of respondents agreed that juveniles convicted of their second or third crime should receive the same punishment as adults convicted of their second or third crime.

In response to this public pressure, many policy makers are backing legislation to make it easier to try juveniles as adults. In proposing one such law, Bill McCollum, a Republican congressman from Florida, stated, "The juvenile justice system isn't working. This bill puts consequences back into the law."[4]

Eliminate the Juvenile Justice System

Because the juvenile justice system is so inadequate to handle today's violent youths, policy makers should consider eliminating the system altogether. Instead of maintaining two separate systems—one for juveniles and one for adults—the two systems could be combined into one system for all age groups. Morgan Reynolds, the director of the Criminal Justice Center at the National Center for Policy Analysis, argues that this reform would be more consistent with the ideal of equal justice for all citizens: "The principles of justice are symbolized by the blindfold, balance scales, and sword of Justitia. One system with equal justice for all—not separate systems for different groups—serves us best."[5] If adults and juveniles were combined in one system, it would still be possible to take the age of the convict into account as a factor during sentencing and to detain teens and adults in separate facilities in order to protect juveniles from predatory adult convicts.

Adult Punishment Is the Only Way

It is obvious that the current system of treating all delinquent juveniles as children who need the support and guidance of concerned professionals is flawed. Many young people do conform to this description. However, many other youths have the capacity to commit repeated acts of violence and show no remorse or potential for rehabilitation. Adult punishment is the only way to protect society from these teens and to deter other youths from following in their footsteps.

1. Suzanne Fields, "Teenage Mischief Becomes Teenage Terror," *Conservative Chronicle,* November 17, 1993, p. 24.

2. Quoted in Ted Gest and Victoria Pope, "Crime Time Bomb," *U.S. News & World Report,* March 25, 1996, p. 30.

3. T. Markus Funk, "Young and Arrestless," *Reason,* February 1996, p. 50.

4. Quoted in Richard Lacayo, "Teen Crime," *Time,* July 21, 1997, p. 28.

5. Morgan Reynolds, "Abolish the Juvenile Justice System?" *Intellectual Ammunition,* November/December 1996. On-line. Internet. Available http://www.heartland.org/ 03nvdc96.htm.

"Teens in adult prisons are not only more likely to become hardened criminals, they are also more likely to be sexually abused, physically beaten, or to commit suicide."

Violent Teens Should Not Be Tried and Sentenced as Adults

Before joining the effort to lock thirteen-year-olds up with adult felons, legislators and citizens would be wise to examine the facts regarding the effectiveness of this policy. As stated by Barry Krisberg, the president of the National Council on Crime and Delinquency, a nonprofit organization that focuses on criminal and juvenile justice policy,

> Few juvenile justice policies have received more political and media attention in recent years than the idea of shifting juveniles to the adult system. Yet there is remarkably little empirical evidence that this approach would produce any positive benefits.[1]

Indeed, the few studies that have been done on the practice of transferring juveniles to criminal court (that is, the adult court system) cast doubt on the ability of this practice to reduce youth violence.

The best study to date was conducted by a team of researchers in Florida in 1996. They compared the rates of recidivism (committing subsequent crimes) of juveniles transferred to adult courts to those of juveniles retained in the juvenile court system. Although the youths who were transferred to adult courts were incarcerated for longer periods of time, according to the researchers, they were more likely to commit new crimes after their release than those who remained in the juvenile system. Youths who were transferred to adult courts also committed worse offenses, and committed them much sooner after their release, than teens released from the juvenile system. Based on their findings, the researchers conclude, "Overall, the results suggest that transfer in Florida had little deterrent value. Nor has it produced any incapacitative benefits that enhance public safety."[2]

More Harm Than Good

Not only is the effectiveness of transferring juveniles to adult courts unproven, there is also considerable evidence that the practice may actually do more harm than good. Teens who are imprisoned along with convicted adult felons are likely to emulate their new peers and be indoctrinated into the criminal lifestyle. As the American Civil Liberties Union states,

> Putting young offenders in adult prisons increases, not lessens, their propensity for committing crime. While in prison, the juvenile offender will learn from older, more hardened criminals. When he is released back into the community in his twenties—undereducated, unsocialized, unemployable, and at the peak of physical power—he will be the very model of the very person we wished most to avoid.[3]

Teens in adult prisons are not only more likely to become hardened criminals, they are also more likely to be sexually abused, physically beaten, or to commit suicide. According to the Children's Defense Fund, an organization that advocates policies to help children,

> The danger is clear: compared to children in juvenile facilities, children in adult jails commit suicide

eight times as often, are five times as likely to be sexually assaulted, and are twice as likely to be beaten by staff. In addition, compared to children in juvenile facilities, children in adult jails are much more likely to be attacked with a weapon.[4]

A vivid illustration of the fate that awaits many juveniles in adult institutions is provided by Bruce Shapiro in the *Nation* magazine. He tells the story of Rodney Hulin Jr. of Beaumont, Texas, who was convicted of arson at the age of sixteen and sentenced to serve eight years in an adult prison:

> Shortly after arriving at the Clemens Unit in Brazoria County, he was raped by another inmate. He asked for protective custody but was turned down. Repeatedly beaten, raped and robbed, Rodney hanged himself; he was in a coma for four months

Eleven-year-old Nathanial James Abraham murdered a stranger outside a convenience store in 1998. The increase in pre-teen violence has led some to propose that more juveniles be tried as adults.

before dying. In one of his last letters he wrote: "Dad, I'm scared, scared that I will die in here."[5]

What happened to Rodney Hulin should not be repeated.

Unfounded Criticism

Many of those who advocate the large-scale transfer of juveniles to adult courts and prisons claim that drastic reform is needed because the juvenile justice system is inherently flawed. Specifically, they contend that the system coddles juveniles by giving them short sentences and erasing their criminal records when they turn eighteen. Opponents are especially critical of the philosophy on which the juvenile justice system is founded. That philosophy holds that youths are different from adults because they are still in the process of developing. Because they are more susceptible to outside influence, the theory goes, they should receive rehabilitation and treatment rather than harsh punishment. Many critics contend that this entire premise is flawed and that the juvenile court is an outdated system that should be eliminated entirely.

These criticisms are invalid. Psychologists are quick to confirm the obvious: Teenagers *are* different from adults. They are more impulsive and have less control over their emotions. They lack a lifetime of experiences to draw from when attempting to make decisions. They need adult support and guidance as well as adult discipline. As the Coalition for Juvenile Justice states,

> The juvenile justice system was established in recognition of the fact that children and adolescents are quite different from adults, not just in size or physical maturity but also developmentally. Young people were deemed to be capable of being rehabilitated and changed.[6]

The view that juveniles are more malleable than adults is as true today as it was when the first juvenile court was established in 1899. Ignoring this crucial distinction does an extreme disservice to America's young people and deprives them of the services they need in order to develop into responsible young men and women.

Not only is the juvenile justice system based on a sound philosophy, but it has also proven itself effective at turning teens' lives around. Rather than detaining—and essentially abandoning—juveniles for the duration of their sentence, the juvenile justice system involves convicted youths in treatment programs designed to alter their behavior by improving their interpersonal skills, self-control, education, and job skills. According to James C. Howell, the former director of the Research and Program Development Division of the OJJDP, such programs have been shown to reduce recidivism by as much as 40 percent, even among the most violent offenders.

Giving Up on the Young

The juvenile justice system is clearly appropriate for even the most violent juvenile offender. The drive to transfer increasing numbers of youths to the adult system—or to abolish the juvenile justice system altogether—is an expression of a collective lack of concern for the young. As Mike Males and Faye Docuyanan write in response to such proposals: "We are giving up on human beings at a younger and younger age."[7] Rather than giving up on teens and consigning them to a fate like that of Rodney Hulin, society should provide them with the help they need in order to make the transition to an adulthood free of crime and violence.

It is society's responsibility to meet the needs of the young. Bypassing or eliminating the juvenile justice system would constitute a failure on the part of the nation to provide teens with the support they need to succeed in life. As Howell writes,

> Those who would abolish the juvenile court fail to realize that it is society's official means of holding itself accountable for the well-being of its children and the family unit. Children are developmentally

different from adults, and therefore children and families need a separate court system to address their legal concerns.[8]

Let's not redefine children as adults to create an illusion of public safety and satisfy our desire for retribution.

1. Barry Krisberg, *The Impact of the Justice System on Serious, Violent, and Chronic Juvenile Offenders*. San Francisco: National Council on Crime and Delinquency, May 1997, p. 19.

2. Donna M. Bishop et al., "The Transfer of Juveniles to Criminal Court: Does It Make a Difference?" *Crime & Delinquency*, April 1996, p. 183.

3. American Civil Liberties Union, "ACLU Fact Sheet on Juvenile Crime," *In Congress*, May 14, 1996. On-line. Internet. Available http://www.aclu.org/congress/juvenile.htm.

4. Children's Defense Fund, "Juvenile Crime Bill Would Harm Children," *Action Alert!* January 15, 1997. On-line. Internet. Available http://www.childrensdefense.org/s10.html.

5. Bruce Shapiro, "The Adolescent Lockup," *Nation*, July 7, 1997, p. 7.

6. Coalition for Juvenile Justice, *No Easy Answers: Juvenile Justice in a Climate of Fear.* Washington, DC: Coalition for Juvenile Justice, 1995.

7. Mike Males and Faye Docuyanan, "Crackdown on Kids: Giving Up on the Young," *Progressive*, February 1996, p. 24.

8. James C. Howell, "Abolish the Juvenile Court? Nonsense!" *Juvenile Justice Update*, February/March 1998, p. 13.

"Keeping teens off the streets late at night is a good way to keep them out of trouble and safe from the threat of violence."

Curfews and Antiloitering Laws Can Prevent Teen Violence

In May 1996, in a speech delivered at the New Orleans Church of God in Christ, President Bill Clinton advocated teen curfews as a way to "bring more order and structure and discipline"[1] to the lives of the nation's young people. Clinton was right.

Common sense alone will tell you that keeping teens off the streets late at night is a good way to keep them out of trouble and safe from the threat of violence. As stated by Jeff Cotner, a police lieutenant in Dallas, "You don't have to be a rocket scientist to figure out that if juveniles are home by midnight, they are less likely to be a victim of crime or involved with folks who are."[2]

What Are Curfews?

The ages and hours governed by curfew laws vary from region to region. The laws generally forbid young people under the age of sixteen or seventeen to be in public between the hours of eleven P.M. and dawn. Some cities give teens an extra hour on Friday and Saturday nights. Exceptions are usually made for teens who need to travel to and from work or other legitimate activities.

In most cities, youths who are picked up for violating a curfew are taken to a central holding area and held until their parents or guardians retrieve them. They are not detained in juvenile hall unless they have been involved in a separate crime in addition to violating the curfew. Some detention centers offer teens counseling services or activities such as basketball or video games.

Many American cities have had curfews on the books for decades. These laws have often gone unenforced because enforcing them requires a great deal of police officers' time. In the early 1990s, however, in response to sharp increases in juvenile crime, cities nationwide began to resurrect their old curfew laws or to pass new ones. As of December 1997, 276 of 347 cities surveyed by the U.S. Conference of Mayors (USCM) had nighttime curfews and 76 had daytime curfews.

Why Are Curfews Necessary?

Some critics believe that curfews represent an intrusion by government into the private realm of family life and violate the rights of parents to raise their children as they see fit. However, curfews are needed precisely because some parents are failing to control their teenage children, placing society at risk of violent juvenile crime. In fairness, other parents are doing a heroic job of trying to reign in adolescents who are simply beyond their control. In either case, invoking curfews to ensure that teens are off the streets and safe at home during high-crime hours is an appropriate use of police power.

Are Curfews Effective?

The effectiveness of curfews was confirmed by a 1997 survey by the USCM. The conference surveyed 347 cities about their use of curfews and their perception of curfews' effectiveness in fighting juvenile crime. According to the survey, 90 percent of the cities with curfews considered enforcing curfews to be a good use of police officers' time; 93 percent considered a curfew a useful tool for police officers.

The USCM reports that city leaders identified a wide range of benefits from curfews. Curfews improve their ability to prevent juvenile crime by allowing them to break up and disperse groups of teens before they have the opportunity to engage in unlawful activity. In addition, curfews give parents both an incentive and a tool for controlling their teenage children. Parents are forced to be more responsible since they are the ones called if a teen is picked up for a violation. However, the curfew law also gives them "a specific reason to tell their children they cannot be out after a certain time."[3] According to the USCM,

> Many respondents felt that curfews represented a proactive way to combat youth violence. They saw curfews as a way to involve parents, as a deterrent to future crime, and as a way to keep juveniles from being victimized. . . . They said that . . . curfews are a good prevention tool, keeping the good kids good and keeping the at-risk kids from becoming victims or victimizers.[4]

One of the biggest contributors to the problem of teen violence is gang activity. In a study by the Office of Juvenile Justice and Delinquency Prevention (OJJDP), juvenile gang members were found to be responsible for twice as many violent crimes as nongang members. Curfews can help the police prevent such violence by forbidding groups of teen gang members from congregating in public. In the USCM study, 83 percent of the cities with curfews indicated that a curfew helps to curb gang violence:

> Officials believe it is a tool to reach "wanna-be" gang members and keep recruitment to a minimum;

it prevents gang members from gathering; it gives the police a legal reason to contact individuals or the group; it tells kids their movements are being monitored and lessens gang activities during the curfew hours.[5]

The results of the USCM survey clearly show that curfews are effective tools in the effort to curb teen violence. Indeed, 53 percent of the cities that have had curfews for ten years or more have seen a reduction in juvenile crime that they attribute directly to curfews.

Are Curfews Constitutional?

Curfews have withstood most challenges, including those claiming that the laws are unconstitutional. The American Civil Liberties Union (ACLU) has challenged curfews in many cities and states, saying the laws violate "minors' fundamental freedoms of movement and expression."[6]

However, a 1993 ruling by the Fifth Circuit Court of Appeals in New Orleans confirmed the constitutionality of curfew laws. In upholding a Dallas curfew, the court ruled that because the law made various exceptions, such as allowing teens to travel to or from work or other legitimate activities, "any burden this ordinance places upon minors' constitutional rights will be minimal."[7] These minor limitations on teens' rights were permissible, the court ruled, because the government had a "compelling interest" in reducing juvenile crime. This ruling clearly shows that curfews are constitutional because the minor restrictions they place on teens' activities are justified by the compelling need to prevent juvenile crime and protect young people from violence.

Antiloitering Laws

In tandem with curfews, many jurisdictions are using additional means of keeping youths—specifically gang members—off the streets. Local leaders are passing antiloitering ordinances and other laws, sometimes called injunctions, that forbid gang members from engaging in particular behaviors, such as gathering in public, wearing gang colors, or possessing heavy chains or tools used for stealing cars.

Gang antiloitering laws have been challenged as being unconstitutional on grounds similar to those leveled against curfews. For example, the ACLU argues that it is unconstitutional to prohibit behavior that is not in itself illegal, such as possessing heavy chains and tools used for stealing cars. However, the possession of weapons and the tools of crime by gang members are used to intimidate and coerce people in the community. As Roger L. Conner, the director of the Center for Community Interest, states,

> The injunctions, by preventing gangsters from flaunting their gang affiliation and congregating in specified public areas, directly attack the sense of collective impunity that drives gang activity. They thus give the community the leverage it needs to face down threats of violence and rebuild a culture of respect.[8]

Antiloitering laws and teen curfews are both valuable tools in the effort to reduce teen violence. If teens are not out on the streets late at night, they will be unable to gather with their peers and prod one another into acts of violence. They will also be less likely to be victimized by violence. Similarly, if gangs are forbidden from assembling in public, they will be unable to recruit new members, to intimidate the public, and to harm one another. In short, they will be more likely to grow into adulthood intact and free of a criminal record. These minor limitations on teens' freedom are a small price to pay for a long, healthy future.

1. Quoted in "The Curfew Card," *Time Daily*, May 31, 1996. On-line. Internet. Available http://cgi.pathfinder.com/time/daily/article/0,1344,6712,00.html.

2. Quoted in Evan Gahr, "Towns Turn Teens into Pumpkins," *Insight*, February 3, 1997, p. 40.

3. U.S. Conference of Mayors, *A Status Report on Youth Curfews in America's Cities: A 347-City Survey*. Washington, DC: United States Conference of Mayors, 1997.

4. U.S. Conference of Mayors, *A Status Report on Youth Curfews in America's Cities*.

5. U.S. Conference of Mayors, *A Status Report on Youth Curfews in America's Cities*.

6. American Civil Liberties Union, "Curfew Overturned in Washington State," press release, June 2, 1997. On-line. Internet. Available from http://www.aclu-wa.org/pubs/releases/970602.shtml.

7. Quoted in "Teen Curfews," *Issues and Controversies On File*, August 30, 1996, p. 533.

8. Roger L. Conner, "A Gangsta's Rights," *Responsive Community*, Winter 1995–1996, p. 56.

"Curfews are fundamentally unfair because they punish all teens for the actions . . . of a few."

Curfews and Antiloitering Laws Are Ineffective and Unconstitutional

Cities nationwide have decided that the best way to keep teens from committing violence is to monitor their activities and regulate their movements. Curfew laws that have been on the books for years are now being enforced for the first time, and new laws are being penned in an effort to keep young people off the streets during the late night–early morning hours— generally eleven P.M. to six A.M. In addition, new antiloitering laws are being passed that make it a crime to be a gang member, to associate with gang members, or even to resemble a gang member while in public.

These crime-fighting tools are touted as the solution to the juvenile crime problem. Proponents insist that keeping teens safe at home will protect them from threats and bar them from the temptations that lurk in the night. While the goal of protecting teens is laudable, a more responsible approach would be to eradicate the threats and temptations rather than imprison teens in their own homes.

Curfews Are Ineffective

The most obvious problem with the concept of nighttime teen curfews is that most juvenile crime occurs after school hours rather than late at night. When asked whether curfew enforcement is a good use of police officers' time, one San Francisco city official stated, "Offenses occur before curfew hours. Therefore, the curfew is ineffective."[1] While some jurisdictions have implemented daytime curfews, these are mostly geared toward reducing truancy during school hours rather than preventing juvenile crime after school.

New Orleans is often cited as a success story for curfews. The juvenile crime rate decreased 27 percent after that city imposed a strict curfew in 1993. In his February 15, 1998, reelection victory speech, Mayor Marc Morial credits the curfew for helping to clean up his city. However, a closer look at the statistics reveals that curfews have not significantly reduced juvenile crime. According to Robert E. Shepherd Jr., a professor of law at the University of Richmond, juvenile crime dropped only 9 percent during curfew hours and increased slightly during noncurfew hours. He concludes that "the total drop in juvenile arrests for serious crime was about

5 percent—the same rate of decrease that had occurred in the city in the previous two years."[2]

Additional evidence of the ineffectiveness of curfews comes from Los Angeles. In February 1998 the Los Angeles Police Department released a report evaluating the effects of a six-month crackdown on curfew violators. The report states that "an examination of the number of crimes that occurred during the curfew enforcement hours revealed that the . . . effort has not greatly impacted the number of minors who became crime victims or the total number of violent crimes committed."[3]

Curfews Are Unconstitutional

Besides being ineffective, curfews are fundamentally unfair because they punish all teens for the actions—or more accurately, the potential actions—of a few. As Shepherd states, "Curfews place not only limitations on the activities of the two-tenths of 1 percent of youth who commit serious offenses, but also on the 99.8 percent who seek to engage in legitimate interests during the nighttime hours."[4] In June 1997 the Washington State Court of Appeals pointed to this inherent unfairness in striking down a curfew law in the community of Bellingham. The court cited past precedent in reaching its decision:

> Noting that the number of juveniles engaged in safe and innocent activity almost certainly outnumbers those engaged in criminal activity, the courts have held that confining all of them to their homes or a few designated activities without evidence that such Draconian restrictions were necessary to address juvenile crime is not a narrowly tailored response to the problem.[5]

Curfews violate several amendments to the Constitution, including the First Amendment, which guarantees citizens the right to peacefully assemble in public. The courts have confirmed that curfews violate teens' rights. In March 1989, in the case of *Waters v. Barry*, the U.S. District Court for the

District of Columbia blocked the implementation of a curfew law. In making his ruling, Judge Charles Richey stated that "the right to walk the streets, or to meet publicly with one's friends for a noble purpose or for no purpose at all—and to do so whenever one pleases—is an integral component of life in a free and ordered society."[6]

Unreasonable Searches and Parents' Rights

Curfews also open the door to violations of the Fourth Amendment, which protects citizens against unreasonable searches and seizures. Armed with the power to stop anyone who looks young, the police can detain teens without probable cause and subject them to frisks and interrogations. This tool will be used disproportionately against minority youths due to the popular stereotype that young minority males are likely to be criminals.

Curfews not only violate the rights of teens, they impinge on the rights of parents as well. By imposing a universal curfew, the government violates parents' Fifth Amendment right to direct their children's upbringing by setting rules that they believe are appropriate. As Michael Evans, a San Diego father who challenged that city's curfew law in 1995, states, "If I think my daughter is mature enough to be out after 10 p.m., then that's my business."[7] In the 1996 case of *Hutchins v. District of Columbia*, the judge expressed a similar sentiment: "These intrusions into the authority of parents to make reasonable rules for their children and to teach their children to mature into responsible and self-reliant adults are an infringement upon parental liberty."[8] Parents, rather than local government, should be free to determine what time their children should be home and in bed.

Antiloitering Laws

Along with curfews, another recent tactic in the fight against teen violence is the enactment of local gang injunctions, also referred to as antiloitering laws and gang ordinances. These laws make it a crime for persons suspected of being gang members to congregate in public or to engage in a wide variety of activities, including wearing gang colors or possessing spray paint (which presumably will be used to deface public property). These laws are unconstitutional for many of the same reasons as curfew laws. Like curfews, they impinge on teens' freedom to exercise their First Amendment right of assembly, and they give the police the green light to search teens without probable cause.

Antiloitering laws especially threaten minority teens. The laws allow police to detain any young person who is reasonably suspected of being a gang member. Due to the racism that pervades the criminal justice system, minority teens—especially in poor urban areas—are often assumed to be gang members by virtue of the color of their skin. Thus the gang ordinances allow police to unfairly target such youths for arrest. As George Brooks, the Chaplain at Chicago's Cook County Jail, astutely observes, "If the ordinance were applied equally in all communities, regardless of race, ethnicity or social status, the country on the whole would be outraged."[9]

Making the Streets Safer

Those who promote antiloitering laws and curfews have good intentions—to prevent teen violence and victimization. The solution to teen violence is not to put teens under house arrest; the solution is to make the streets safer.

1. Quoted in U. S. Conference of Mayors, *A Status Report on Youth Curfews in America's Cities: A 347-City Survey*. Washington, DC: U. S. Conference of Mayors, 1997.

2. Robert E. Shepherd Jr., "The Proliferation of Juvenile Curfews," American Bar Association Criminal Justice Section, Juvenile Justice Center, n.d. On-line. Internet. Available http://www.abanet.org/crimjust/juvjus/cjcurfew.html.

3. Quoted in Matt Lait, "Study Finds Curfew Law Fails to Curb Violent Crime," *Los Angeles Times*, February 10, 1998.

4. Shepherd, "The Proliferation of Juvenile Curfews."

5. American Civil Liberties Union, "Curfew Overturned in Washington State," press release, June 2, 1997. On-line. Internet. Available http://www.aclu-wa.org/pubs/releases/970602.shtml.

6. Quoted in "Teen Curfews," *Issues and Controversies On File*, August 30, 1996, p. 533.

7. Quoted in "Teen Curfews," *Issues and Controversies On File*.

8. Quoted in Shepherd, "The Proliferation of Juvenile Curfews."

9. George Brooks, "Let's Not Gang Up on Kids," *U.S. Catholic*, March 1997, p. 19.

APPENDIX A

Related Documents

Document 1: Trends in Violent Teen Crime

The following excerpt from a report published by the Office of Juvenile Justice and Delinquency Prevention details the increase in violent juvenile crime from 1985 through 1994. It also points out that such crime decreased in 1995, a trend that continued through 1996.

By the early 1990's, rates of criminal violence, including youth violence, reached unparalleled levels in American society. Compared to adolescents in other countries, American teenagers exhibit alarmingly high rates of violence. For example, an American 17-year-old is 10 times more likely to commit murder than his or her Canadian counterpart.

Criminologists now question the conventional wisdom that young adults represent the most violence-prone age group. In recent years, teenagers have so accelerated their rate of involvement that in 1994 teens ages 15 to 17 slightly exceeded the arrest rate of young adults ages 18 to 20 for Violent Crime Index offenses. Increased youth involvement in violence is clearly evident from an analysis of official juvenile offending rates and victimization trends over the past decade.

The first statistical trends to consider are those regarding juveniles arrested for Violent Crime Index offenses, that is, murder and nonnegligent manslaughter, forcible rape, robbery, and aggravated assault. From 1986 to 1995, juvenile arrests for Violent Crime Index offenses increased 67 percent, with changes in specific crime rates as shown below:

- Juvenile arrests for murder and nonnegligent manslaughter increased 90 percent.
- Juvenile arrests for forcible rape declined 4 percent. Juvenile arrests for robbery increased 63 percent.
- Juvenile arrests for aggravated assault increased 78 percent.

Second, while boys still account for more than their share of serious violence, statistical evidence indicates that girls are increasingly involved in aggressive crimes:

- In 1995, females were responsible for 15 percent of the total juvenile arrests for Violent Crime Index offenses, with the most extensive involvement in aggravated assault arrests (20 percent).
- From 1991 to 1995, female juvenile arrests for Violent Crime Index offenses increased 34 percent, nearly four times the male juvenile increase of 9 percent.

Third, 1994 data from the "National Crime Victimization Survey" (Bureau of Justice Statistics, unpublished tables) demonstrate how frequently youth are victims of the violent crimes of simple and aggravated assault, rape, and robbery:

- A total of 2.6 million violent crimes were committed against juveniles ages 12 to 17, representing a 44-percent increase since 1984.
- Among 12- to 17-year-olds, boys were one and one-half times more likely to be victims of violent crimes than girls.
- Younger adolescents ages 12 to 14 were equally at risk for violent victimization as older adolescents ages 15 to 17. Nearly 12 percent of all adolescents were victims of violent crime in 1994.

Fourth, it is instructive to examine trends regarding juveniles who are homicide victims:

- The number of juveniles murdered increased 82 percent between 1984 and 1994. A daily average of seven juveniles were homicide victims in 1994. This means that each week about 50 families lost a child to violence.
- From 1984 to 1994, juvenile homicide victimizations involving firearms nearly tripled, while those not involving firearms remained constant.

Although youth violence affects all segments of American society, it has particularly devastating effects on the African-American community, as the following statistics show:

- In 1994, African-American juveniles were six times more likely than Caucasian juveniles to be homicide victims.
- Homicides involving firearms have been the leading cause of death for African-American males ages 15 through 19 since 1969, and the rates have more than doubled from 1979 to 1989.
- Since 1987, African Americans have outnumbered Caucasians as juvenile homicide offenders. By 1994, 61 percent of juvenile homicide offenders were African American and 36 percent were Caucasian.

By any reasonable standard, current national rates of youth violence are unacceptably high. Projections of dramatic increases in juvenile violent crime arrests in the next century are cause for even greater concern. However, there is some recent good news about the juvenile violent crime arrest rate. In 1995, for the first year in nearly a decade, the number of juvenile arrests for Violent Crime Index offenses declined. The 3-percent decrease included a 14-percent decline in juvenile arrests for murder and nonnegligent manslaughter, a 4-percent decline in forcible rape, a 1-percent decline in robbery, and a 3-percent decline in aggravated assault from 1994 to 1995.

Barbara Tatem Kelley et al., *Epidemiology of Serious Violence.* Washington, DC: Office of Juvenile Justice and Delinquency Prevention, June 1997. On-line. Internet. Available http://www.ncjrs.org/txtfiles1/165152.txt.

Document 2: "The Young and the Ruthless"

James Alan Fox writes that the high rate of violent juvenile crime bodes ill for the nation's future.

Judging from countless media reports in newspapers from coast to coast, it would surely seem that we have finally gotten a handle on the Nation's crime problem. The FBI release of crime statistics for 1995 revealed a welcome drop in violent crime, including an 8 percent decline in homicide. After four straight years of lower crime levels, some crime experts and law enforcement officials have even dared boldly to suggest that we're winning the war against crime.

Though recent trends are encouraging, at least superficially, there is little time to celebrate these successes. It is doubtful that today's improving crime picture will last for very long. Most likely, this is the calm before the crime storm. While many police officials can legitimately feel gratified about that arrested crime rate—better that it be down than up—there is much more to the great crime drop story. Hidden beneath the overall drop in homicide and other violent crime is a soaring rate of mayhem among teenagers.

There are actually two crime trends ongoing in America—one for the young and one for the mature, which are moving in opposite directions. Since 1990, for example, the rate of homicide committed by adults, ages 25 and older, has declined 18 percent as the baby boomers matured well past their crime prime years. At the same time, however, the homicide rate by teenagers, ages 14 to 17, has increased 22 percent. Even more alarming and tragic is that over the past decade, the homicide rate at the hands of teenagers has nearly tripled, increasing 172 percent from 1985 to 1994.

Therefore, while the overall U.S. homicide rate has indeed declined in recent years, the rate of juvenile murder continues to grow, unabated by the spread of community policing, increased incarceration, and a variety of other popular crime-fighting strategies. In the overall crime mix, the sharp decline in crime among the large adult population has eclipsed the rising crime rate among the relatively small population of teens.

Trends in age-specific violent arrest rates for homicide, rape, robbery, and aggravated assault confirm the patterns found in homicide statistics. Teenagers now exceed all age groups, even young adults, in their absolute rate of arrest for violent crime overall. Conventional wisdom in criminology—that young adults generally represent the most violence-prone group—apparently needs to be modified in light of these disturbing changes.

The causes of the surge in youth violence since the mid-1980s reach, of course, well beyond demographics. There have been tremendous changes in the social context of crime over the past decade, which explain why this generation of youth—the young and the ruthless—is more violent than others before it. Our youngsters have more dangerous drugs in their bodies, more deadly weapons in their hands, and a seemingly more casual attitude about violence. It is clear that too many teenagers in this country, particularly those in urban areas, are plagued with idleness and even hopelessness. A growing number of teens and preteens see few feasible or attractive alternatives to violence, drug use, and gang membership. For them, the American Dream is a nightmare. There may be little to live for and to strive for, but plenty to die for and even to kill for.

The problem of kids with guns cannot be overstated in view of recent trends in gun-related killings among youth. Since the mid-1980s, the number of gun-homicides—particularly with handguns—perpetrated by juveniles has quadrupled, while the prevalence of juvenile homicide involving all other weapons combined has remained virtually constant.

Guns are far more lethal in several respects. A 14-year-old armed with a gun is far more menacing than a 44-year-old with a gun. Although juveniles may be untrained in using firearms, they are more willing to pull the trigger over trivial matters—a leather jacket, a pair of sneakers, a challenging remark, or no reason at all—without fully considering the consequences. Also, the gun psychologically distances the offender from the victim; if the same youngster had to kill his or her victim (almost always someone known) with hands, he or she might be deterred by the physical contact. . . .

As if the situation with youth violence was not bad enough already, future demographics are expected to make matters even worse. Not only are today's violent teens maturing into more violent young adults, but they are being succeeded by a new and large group of teenagers. The same massive baby-boom cohort that as teenagers produced a crime wave in the 1970s has since grown up and had children of their own. There are now 39 million children in this country under the age of 10, more young children than at any time since the 1950s when the original baby boomers were in grade school. The newest group of youngsters—the baby boomerang cohort—will soon reach their adolescence.

By the year 2005, the number of teens, ages 14 to 17, will swell by 17 percent, with an even larger increase among people of color—20 percent among African-Americans and 30 percent among Latinos. Given the difficult conditions in which many of these youngsters grow up—with inferior schools and violence-torn neighborhoods—many more teenagers will be at risk in the years ahead.

Tragically, the number of violent teens has grown in recent years, even as the population of teenagers has contracted. But the teen population has bottomed out and is now on the upswing. If current rates of offending remain unchanged, the number of teens who commit murder and other serious violent crimes shall increase, if only because of the demographic turnaround in the population at risk. However, given the worsening conditions in which children are being raised, given the breakdown of all our institutions as well as of our cultural norms, given our wholesale disinvestment in youth, our nation faces the grim prospect of a future wave of juvenile violence that may make the 1990s look like "the good old days."

James Alan Fox, "Should the Federal Government Have a Major Role in Reducing Juvenile Crime? Pro," *Congressional Digest*, August/September 1996.

Document 3: Kids and Guns

Stuart Greenbaum reports on the growing availability of guns in America and its impact on teen violence.

Late in 1996 an 11-year-old boy was shot and killed. An 18-year-old allegedly killed the boy because he had shorted him on drug money. The shooting should have rocked the Chicago neighborhood where it took place, except that this kind of thing happens all too often.

The lethal mix of children and guns has reached a crisis in the United States. Teenage boys are more likely to die of gunshot wounds than from all natural causes combined. The number of children dying from gunshot wounds and the number of children committing homicides continue to rise at alarming rates.

Guns are now the weapon of choice for youth. Gun homicides by juveniles have tripled since 1983, while homicides involving other weapons have declined. From 1983 through 1995, the proportion of homicides in which a juvenile used a gun increased from 55 percent to 80 percent.

Disputes that would previously have ended in fist fights are now more likely to lead to shootings. A 1993 Louis Harris poll showed that 35 percent of children ages 6 to 12 fear their lives will be cut short by gun violence. A 1990 Centers for Disease Control and Prevention study found that one in five 9th through 12th graders reported carrying a weapon in the past month; one in five of those carried a firearm.

"No corner of America is safe from increasing levels of criminal violence, including violence committed by and against juveniles," Attorney General Janet Reno has observed. "Parents are afraid to let their children walk to school alone. Children hesitate to play in neighborhood playgrounds. The elderly lock themselves in their homes, and innocent Americans of all ages find their lives changed by the fear of crime.

The number of murdered juveniles increased 47 percent between 1980 and 1994, according to figures from Juvenile Offenders and Victims: 1996 Update on Violence. The Summary, which cites data from the Federal Bureau of Investigation's Uniform Crime Reporting Program, notes that from 1980 through 1994 an estimated 326,170 persons were murdered in the United States. Of these, 9 percent (30,200) were youth under age 18. While there was a 1-percent increase from 1980 through 1994 in the total number of murders, the rate of juveniles murdered increased from five per day to seven per day. Fifty-three percent of the juveniles killed in 1994 were teenagers ages 15 to 17, while 30 percent were younger than age 6. In 1994, one in five murdered juveniles was killed by a juvenile offender.

Recently, however, there has been good news. Between 1994 and 1995, juvenile arrests for murder declined 14 percent, resulting in the number of juvenile murder arrests in 1995 being 9 percent below the 1991 figure. Overall arrests for violent juvenile crime decreased 3 percent between 1994 and 1995—the first decline in 9 years. These efforts must continue, however, as even these reduced rates are substantially higher than 1986 levels. . . .

Guns are readily available to juveniles. Although Federal law mandates that a person must be at least 18 years old to purchase a shotgun or rifle, and at least 21 years old to buy a handgun, law enforcement officials and youth themselves report that buying guns illegally is relatively easy for juveniles. Increasingly, juveniles believe they need guns for protection or carry them as status symbols. As more guns appear in the community, a local arms race ensues. . . .

As disturbing as youth gun violence is, it need not be inevitable. It is preventable—as many programs throughout the United States are beginning to demonstrate. With the public alarmed about the problem, public servants and practitioners might bear in mind the Greek philosopher Solon's words, "There can be no justice until those of us who are unaffected by crime become as indignant as those who are."

Stuart Greenbaum, "Kids and Guns: From Playgrounds to Battlegrounds," *Juvenile Justice*, September 1997.

Document 4: The Abandonment of Young People

Luis J. Rodriguez criticizes society's tendency to view teenagers as "super-predators" and challenges adults to become more involved in the lives of young people.

We are in a disturbing and dangerous time in our development as a people and a nation. A *Chicago Tribune* article by Michael Dorning that appeared on May 7, 1997, was entitled, "U.S. Rewrites the Rules on Youth Justice." The lead paragraph declared "After a decade of escalating youth violence, the political consensus developing in favor of fundamental national changes in juvenile justice comes down to this. A child stops being a child when he picks up a gun."

The article explained how congressional Republicans and Democrats, as well as the Clinton administration, united in supporting new federal laws that would incorporate tougher approaches from various states in dealing with youth crime (for example, by mid-1997, 41 states had passed laws making it easier to try juveniles as adults, according to the National Center for Juvenile Justice in Pittsburgh). California Governor Pete Wilson, in a state that already has the highest incarceration rate in the world, had a month earlier suggested that people as young as 13 be subject to the death penalty.

"In the case of violent offenders or those involved in the drug trade, the young no longer would be viewed as more redeemable than adults," stated

Representative Bill McCollum (R-Fla.) in the Dorning article. "These are people who we want incapacitated. These are violent predator youth."

This has become the prevalent thinking permeating all aspects of our society. Schools, law enforcement, youth agencies, child protective services, and even religious institutions are becoming entangled in a web of policies and directives to turn our backs on a significant section of young people.

We need, therefore, a broad and encompassing national debate on all the issues surrounding youth and violence in this country. It is time we challenged the concepts that young people are unredeemable, that "super-predators" are prepared to overrun our streets in a generation or two, and that the only way to be safe is to build more prisons, institute "zero tolerance" wherever youth encounter programs, and take the "deviants" from our midst.

The net effect of all this pressure is that more and more adults are being forced to remove themselves from authentic and respectful relations with children and adolescents. "Professionalism" has come to mean "don't get involved," particularly in the emotional life of a child. The threads of community are being severed at a time when we need to reconnect them more than ever.

We are seeing the wholesale abandonment of young people, particularly those most in need of guidance, resources, patience, and caring. . . .

It is time to walk with the young people again. To influence them, you must relate to them. To relate to them, you must listen and understand. To understand, you must be where they are going. This is not about "saving" youth—only they can save themselves. Yet by seeing the courage, intelligence, enlightenment, and levels of attention we can provide to them, they may learn what they have to do for themselves, their children, their neighbors, their community.

People can change. This is one of the ideas we have to elucidate as widely as possible. When lawmakers say a child is "unredeemable" at age 16 or 13 or even 10, they are setting in concrete the mental and emotional state of a person that is, in reality, always in flux.

Luis J. Rodriguez, "Hearts and Hands: A New Paradigm for Work with Youth and Violence," *Social Justice*, Winter 1997.

Document 5: The Harmful Effects of Family Breakup

In the following excerpt, author Barbara Dafoe Whitehead asserts that the rising rates of divorce and out-of-wedlock childbirth have contributed to America's social problems—including juvenile crime and school violence.

Divorce and out-of-wedlock childbirth are transforming the lives of American children. In the postwar generation more than 80 percent of children grew up in a family with two biological parents who were married to each other. By 1980 only 50 percent could expect to spend their entire childhood in an intact family. If current trends continue, less than half of all children born today will live continuously with their own mother and father throughout childhood. Most American children will spend several years in a single-mother family. Some will eventually live in stepparent families, but because stepfamilies are more likely to break up than intact (by which I mean two-biological-parent) families, an increasing number of children will experience family breakup two or even three times during childhood.

According to a growing body of social-scientific evidence, children in families disrupted by divorce and out-of-wedlock birth do worse than children in intact families on several measures of well-being. Children in single-parent families are six times as likely to be poor. They are also likely to stay poor longer. Twenty-two percent of children in one-parent families will experience poverty during childhood for seven years or more, as compared with only two percent of children in two-parent families. A 1988 survey by the National Center for Health Statistics found that children in single-parent families are two to three times as likely as children in two-parent families to have emotional and behavioral problems. They are also more likely to drop out of high school, to get pregnant as teenagers, to abuse drugs, and to be in trouble with the law. Compared with children in intact families, children from disrupted families are at a much higher risk for physical or sexual abuse.

Contrary to popular belief, many children do not "bounce back" after divorce or remarriage. Difficulties that are associated with family breakup often persist into adulthood. Children who grow up in single-parent or stepparent families are less successful as adults, particularly in the two domains of life—love and work—that are most essential to happiness. Needless to say, not all children experience such negative effects. However, research shows that many children from disrupted families have a harder time achieving intimacy in a relationship, forming a stable marriage, or even holding a steady job. . . .

Family disruption would be a serious problem even if it affected only individual children and families. But its impact is far broader. Indeed, it is not an exaggeration to characterize it as a central cause of many of our most vexing social problems. Consider three problems that most Americans believe rank among the nation's pressing concerns: poverty, crime, and declining school performance.

More than half of the increase in child poverty in the 1980s is attributable to changes in family structure, according to David Eggebeen and Daniel Lichter, of Pennsylvania State University. In fact, if family structure in the United States had remained relatively constant since 1960, the rate of child poverty would be a third lower than it is today. This does not bode well for the future. With more than half of today's children likely to live in single-parent families, poverty and associated welfare costs threaten to become even heavier burdens on the nation.

Crime in American cities has increased dramatically and grown more violent over recent decades. Much of this can be attributed to the rise in disrupted families. Nationally, more than 70 percent of all juveniles in state reform institutions come from fatherless homes. A number of scholarly studies find that even after the groups of subjects are controlled for income, boys from single-mother homes are significantly more likely than others to commit crimes and to wind up in the juvenile justice, court, and penitentiary systems. One such study summarizes the relationship between crime and one-parent families in this way: "The relationship is so strong that controlling for family configuration erases the relationship between race and crime and between low income and crime. This conclusion shows up time and again in the literature." The nation's mayors, as well as police officers, social workers, probation officers, and court officials, consistently point to family breakup as the most important source of rising rates of crime.

Terrible as poverty and crime are, they tend to be concentrated in inner cities and isolated from the everyday experience of many Americans. The same cannot be said of the problem of declining school performance. Nowhere has the impact of family breakup been more profound or widespread than in the nation's public schools. There is a strong consensus that the schools are failing in their historic mission to prepare every American child to be a good worker and a good citizen. And nearly everyone agrees that the schools must undergo dramatic reform in order to reach that goal. In pursuit of that goal, moreover, we have suffered no shortage of bright ideas or pilot projects or bold experiments in school reform. But there is little evidence that measures such as curricular reform, school-based management, and school choice will address, let alone solve, the biggest problem schools face: the rising number of children who come from disrupted families.

The great educational tragedy of our time is that many American children are failing in school not because they are intellectually or physically impaired but because they are emotionally incapacitated. In schools across the nation principals report a dramatic rise in the aggressive, acting-out behavior characteristic of children, especially boys, who are living in single-parent families. The discipline problems in today's suburban schools—assaults on teachers, unprovoked attacks on other students, screaming outbursts in class—outstrip the problems that were evident in the toughest city schools a generation ago. Moreover, teachers find many children emotionally distracted, so upset and preoccupied by the explosive drama of their own family lives that they are unable to concentrate on such mundane matters as multiplication tables.

In response, many schools have turned to therapeutic remediation. A growing proportion of many school budgets is devoted to counseling and other psychological services. The curriculum is becoming more therapeutic: children are taking courses in self-esteem, conflict resolution, and aggression management. Parental advisory groups are conscientiously debating alternative approaches to traditional school discipline, ranging from teacher training in mediation to the introduction of metal detectors and security guards in the schools. Schools are increasingly becoming emergency rooms of the emotions, devoted not only to developing minds but also to repairing hearts. As a result, the mission of the school, along with the culture of the classroom, is slowly changing. What we are seeing, largely as a result of the new burdens of family disruption, is the psychologization of American education. . . .

All this evidence gives rise to an obvious conclusion: growing up in an intact two-parent family is an important source of advantage for American children. Though far from perfect as a social institution, the intact family offers children greater security and better outcomes than its fast-growing alternatives: single-parent and stepparent families. Not only does the intact family protect the child from poverty and economic insecurity; it also provides greater noneconomic investments of parental time, attention, and emotional support over the entire life course. This does not mean that all two-parent families are better for children than all single parent families. But in the face of the evidence it becomes increasingly difficult to sustain the proposition that all family structures produce equally good outcomes for children.

Barbara Dafoe Whitehead, "Dan Quayle Was Right," *Atlantic Monthly*, April 1993.

Document 6: Family Breakup and Social Pathologies: Correlation Versus Causation

Arlene Skolnick and Stacey Rosencranz respond to the argument that the rise in single-parent families has contributed to social problems—including teen violence—in the United States. They contend that social science research does not support the conclusions of the "family restorationists" (those who wish to restore the traditional two-parent family structure). While the research does show a correlation *between family breakdown and social problems, Skolnick and Rosencranz maintain, it does not show that family breakdown is the* cause *of such problems.*

To decide what policies would improve children's lives, we need to answer a number of prior questions:

- Are children who grow up in a one-parent home markedly worse off than those who live with both parents?
- If such children are so disadvantaged, is the source of their problems family structure or some other factor that may have existed earlier or be associated with it? . . .
- Finally, is there a direct link, as so many believe, between family structure and what a *Newsweek* writer calls a "nauseating buffet" of social pathologies, especially crime, violence, and drugs? . . .

The family restorationists do not provide clear answers to these questions. And the answers found in the research literature do not support their extreme statements about the consequences of family structure or some of the drastic policies they propose to change it.

Of course, it's always possible to raise methodological questions about a line of research or to interpret findings in more ways than one. The perfect study, like the perfect crime, is an elusive goal. But some of the family restorationists seem to misunderstand the social science enterprise in ways that seriously undermine their conclusions. For example, they trumpet findings about correlations between family structure and poverty, or lower academic achievement, or behavior problems, as proof of their arguments. Doing so, however, ignores the principle taught in elementary statistics that correlation does not prove causation.

For example, suppose we find that increased ice cream consumption is correlated with increases in drownings. The cause, of course, has nothing to do with ice cream but everything to do with the weather: people swim more and eat more ice cream in the summer. Similarly, single parenthood may be correlated with many problems affecting children, but the causes may lie elsewhere—for example, in economic and emotional problems affecting parents that lead to difficulties raising children and greater chances of divorce. Making it hard for such parents to divorce may no more improve the children's lives than banning ice cream would reduce drowning. Also, causation can and often does go in two directions. Poor women are more likely to have out-of-wedlock babies — this is one of the oldest correlates of poverty — but raising the child may impede them from escaping poverty. In short, finding a correlation between two variables is only a starting point for further analysis.

Arlene Skolnick and Stacey Rosencranz, "The New Crusade for the Old Family," *American Prospect*, Summer 1994.

Document 7: The National Television Violence Study

The National Television Violence Study (NTVS) is an ongoing project being conducted by Mediascope and researchers at four universities. In the "Summary of Findings and Recommendations" for the first year of the study, excerpted below, the NTVS reports that the majority of television shows contain violence and that the context in which such violence is portrayed poses risks to viewers.

CONTENT ANALYSIS OF VIOLENCE
IN TELEVISION PROGRAMMING

This study is based on the largest and most representative sample of television ever examined using scientific content analysis procedures. Researchers randomly selected programs on 23 television channels over a 20 week period to create a composite week of content for each source. The study monitored programs between the hours of 6:00 A.M. and 11:00 P.M., a total of 17 hours a day across seven days of the week, yielding a sum of approximately 119 hours per channel. In total, this project examined approximately 2,500 hours of television programming that includes 2,693 programs; 384 of these were reality-based shows.

KEY FINDINGS

- *The context in which most violence is presented on television poses risks for viewers.* The majority of programs analyzed in this study contain some violence. But more important than the prevalence of violence is the contextual pattern in which most of it is shown. The risks of viewing the most common depictions of televised violence include learning to behave violently, becoming more desensitized to the harmful consequences of violence, and becoming more fearful of being attacked. The contextual patterns noted below are found consistently across most channels, program types, and times of day. Thus, there are substantial risks of harmful effects from viewing violence throughout the television environment.

- *Perpetrators go unpunished in 73% of all violent scenes.* This pattern is highly consistent across different types of programs and channels. The portrayal of rewards and punishments is probably the most important of all contextual factors for viewers as they interpret the meaning of what they see on television. When violence is presented without punishment, viewers are more likely to learn the lesson that violence is successful.

- *The negative consequences of violence are not often portrayed in violent programming.* Most violent portrayals do not show the victim experiencing any serious physical harm or pain at the time the violence occurs. For example, 47% of all violent interactions show no harm to victims, and 58% show no pain. Even less frequent is the depiction of any long-term consequences of violence. In fact, only 16% of all programs portray the long-term negative repercussions of violence, such as psychological, financial, or emotional harm.

- *One out of four violent interactions on television (25%) involve the use of a handgun.* Depictions of violence with guns and other conventional weapons can instigate or trigger aggressive thoughts and behaviors.

- *Only 4% of violent programs emphasize an anti-violence theme.* Very few violent programs place emphasis on condemning the use of violence or on presenting alternatives to using violence to solve problems. This pattern is consistent across different types of programs and channels.

- *On the positive side, television violence is usually not explicit or graphic.* Most violence is presented without any close-up focus on aggressive behaviors and without showing any blood and gore. In particular, less than 3% of violent scenes feature close-ups on the violence and only 15% of scenes contain blood and gore. Explicit or graphic violence contributes to desensitization and can enhance fear.

- *There are some notable differences in the presentation of violence across television channels.* Public broadcasting presents violent programs least often (18%) and those violent depictions that appear pose the least risk of harmful effects. Premium cable channels present the highest percentage of violent programs (85%) and those depictions often pose a greater risk of harm than do most violent portrayals. Broadcast networks present violent programs less frequently (44%) than the industry norm (57%), but when they present violence its contextual features are just as problematic as those on most other channels.
- *There are also some important differences in the presentation of violence across types of television programs.* Movies are more likely to present violence in realistic settings (85%), and to include blood and gore in violent scenes (28%) than other program types. The contextual pattern of violence in children's programming also poses concern. Children's programs are the least likely of all genres to show the long-term negative consequences of violence (5%), and they frequently portray violence in a humorous context (67%).

"Summary of Findings and Recommendations," *National Television Violence Study, 1994–1995.* On-line. Internet. Available http://www.mediascope.org/ntvssmfn.htm.

Document 8: The Unproven Link Between Violence in the Media and Violence in Society

The evidence that violence on television causes real-life violence is unconvincing, according to Jonathan Freedman.

In laboratory tests of this thesis [that watching television violence causes aggression], some children are shown violent programs, others are shown nonviolent programs, and their aggressiveness is measured immediately afterward. The results, although far from consistent, generally show some increase in aggression after a child watches a violent program. Like most laboratory studies of real-world conditions, however, these findings have limited value. In the first place, most of the studies have used dubious measures of aggression. In one experiment, for example, children were asked, "If I had a balloon, would you want me to prick it?" Other measures have been more plausible, but none is unimpeachable. Second, there is the problem of distinguishing effects of violence from effects of interest and excitement. In general, the violent films in these experiments are more arousing than the neutral films. Anyone who is aroused will display more of almost any behavior; there is nothing special about aggression in this respect. Finally and most important, these experiments are seriously contaminated by what psychologists call demand characteristics of the situation: the familiar fact that people try to do what the experimenter wants. Since the children know the experimenter has chosen the violent film, they may assume that they are being given permission to be aggressive.

The simplest way to conduct a real-world study is to find out whether children who watch more violent television are also more aggressive. They are, but the correlations are small, accounting for only 1% to 10% of individual differences in children's aggressiveness. In any case, correlations do not prove causality. Boys watch more TV football than girls, and they play more football than girls, but no one, so far as I know, believes that television is what makes boys more interested in football. Probably personality characteristics that make children more aggressive also make them prefer violent television programs.

Jonathan Freedman, "Violence in the Mass Media and Violence in Society: The Link Is Unproven," *Harvard Mental Health Letter*, May 1996. On-line. Internet. Available http://www.mentalhealth.com/mag1/p5h-vio4.html.

Document 9: The Juvenile Justice and Delinquency Prevention Act

The Juvenile Justice and Delinquency Prevention Act of 1974 created the Department of Juvenile Justice and Delinquency Prevention and established delinquency prevention programs nationwide. The following excerpt explains the law's purpose.

SUBCHAPTER I—GENERALLY
42 U.S.C. 5601 Sec. 101. Congressional statement of findings

(a) The Congress hereby finds that—

(1) juveniles accounted for almost half the arrests for serious crimes in the United States in 1974 and for less than one-third of such arrests in 1983;

(2) recent trends show an upsurge in arrests of adolescents for murder, assault, and weapon use;

(3) the small number of youth who commit the most serious and violent offenses are becoming more violent;

(4) understaffed, overcrowded juvenile courts, prosecutorial and public defender offices, probation services, and correctional facilities and inadequately trained staff in such courts, services, and facilities are not able to provide individualized justice or effective help;

(5) present juvenile courts, foster and protective care programs, and shelter facilities are inadequate to meet the needs of children, who, because of this failure to provide effective services, may become delinquents;

(6) existing programs have not adequately responded to the particular problems of the increasing numbers of young people who are addicted to or who abuse alcohol and other drugs, particularly nonopiate or polydrug abusers;

(7) juvenile delinquency can be reduced through programs designed to keep students in elementary and secondary schools through the prevention of unwarranted and arbitrary suspensions and expulsions;

(8) States and local communities which experience directly the devastating failures of the juvenile justice system do not presently have sufficient technical expertise or adequate resources to deal comprehensively with the problems of juvenile delinquency;

(9) existing Federal programs have not provided the direction, coordination, resources, and leadership required to meet the crisis of delinquency;

(10) the juvenile justice system should give additional attention to the problem of juveniles who commit serious crimes, with particular attention given to the areas of sentencing, providing resources necessary for informed dispositions, and rehabilitation;

(11) emphasis should be placed on preventing youth from entering the juvenile justice system to begin with; and

(12) the incidence of juvenile delinquency can be reduced through public recreation programs and activities designed to provide youth with social skills, enhance self esteem, and encourage the constructive use of discretionary time.

(b) Congress finds further that the high incidence of delinquency in the United States today results in enormous annual cost and immeasurable loss of human life, personal security, and wasted human resources and that juvenile delinquency constitutes a growing threat to the national welfare requiring immediate and comprehensive action by the Federal Government to reduce and prevent delinquency.

Juvenile Justice and Delinquency Prevention Act, as amended. On-line. Internet. Available http://www. ncjrs.org/txtfiles/ojjjjact.txt

Document 10: The National Juvenile Justice Action Plan

The Coordinating Council on Juvenile Justice and Delinquency Prevention was established in 1992 to coordinate federal programs pertaining to juvenile delinquency prevention, the detention and care of unaccompanied juveniles, and missing and exploited children. The following excerpt presents the eight objectives of the council's National Juvenile Justice Action Plan. The council calls for a blend of punitive measures, such as trying juveniles in criminal (adult) courts, and preventive efforts like mentoring and community mobilization.

Objective 1. Provide immediate intervention and appropriate sanctions and treatment for delinquent juveniles.

Safe communities and juvenile accountability are central to the Action Plan. It proposes a strong juvenile justice system that provides a continuum of services for juveniles who come into the system for a variety of reasons, such as truancy, homelessness, drug abuse, mental illness, or delinquent offenses. The juvenile justice system must be given the tools to assess the risk the juvenile offender poses to the community, determine rehabilitative needs, and provide graduated sanctions and treatment commensurate with both conduct and needs. It must also be able to meet the needs of dependent, abused, and neglected children and status offenders. . . .

A system of graduated sanctions is the recommended mechanism for attaining treatment and accountability goals for delinquent offenders. Graduated sanctions encompass three levels:

- Immediate intervention (community restitution, day treatment centers, diversion programs, and protective supervision projects) for first-time delinquent offenders and many nonviolent repeat offenders.

- Intermediate sanctions (residential and nonresidential community-based programs, weekend detention, intensive supervision, probation, wilderness programs, and boot camps) for many first-time serious and repeat offenders and some violent offenders.
- Secure confinement (community confinement in small, secure treatment facilities or, where necessary, incarceration in training schools, camps, and ranches) for offenders categorized as violent or repeat serious offenders.

Levels of sanctions should be based on consideration of the offense and offense history (risk) and the offender's treatment and rehabilitation needs. . . .

Objective 2. Prosecute certain serious, violent, and chronic juvenile offenders in criminal court.
The purpose of this objective is both to protect the public and to separate certain serious, violent, and chronic juvenile offenders from those juveniles who can benefit from treatment and rehabilitation in the juvenile justice system. Statistics show that a small percentage of the juvenile offender population is responsible for most of the serious and violent juvenile crime. Transferring to criminal court those targeted juvenile offenders who are the most chronic and who commit the most serious and violent crimes enables the juvenile justice system to focus its efforts and resources on the much larger group of at-risk youth and less serious and violent offenders who can benefit from a wide range of effective intervention strategies.

However, States and the Federal Government should review their statutory transfer mechanisms to ensure that they are appropriately applied. The transfer alternative should only be considered for those juveniles whose criminal history, failure to respond to treatment, or serious or violent conduct clearly demonstrates that they require criminal justice system sanctions.

We must also remain vigilant about a juvenile's right to effective counsel and cognizant of the potentially harmful impact of placing juveniles in adult jails, lockups, and correctional facilities, including problems associated with overcrowding, abuse, youth suicide, and the risk of transforming treatable juveniles into hardened criminals. Most of all, a recognition of the continuing need for transfer of juveniles to criminal court must strengthen our resolve to prevent delinquency and intervene early to decrease the risk of future criminal conduct. . . .

Objective 3. Reduce youth involvement with guns, drugs, and gangs.
State and local actions to address gun, drug, and gang violence require a combination of tough and smart law enforcement and prevention activities including: seizing firearms from juvenile offenders in school and turning them over to appropriate law enforcement agencies for tracing; support-

ing technological innovations in gun and ammunition manufacturing that will help reduce the accessibility of lethal weapons; developing appropriate intervention programs for gang-involved youth; and involving youth in planning and implementing youth-focused community oriented policing programs. The Action Plan also supports advances in drug and alcohol prevention and treatment strategies as effective anti-violence strategies. . . .

Objective 4. Provide opportunities for children and youth.
Comprehensive neighborhood-based programs that help children develop positive life skills and minimize risk factors, give them support and direction, and create opportunities for community involvement and service have proven to be the most effective defense against violent delinquency. Additionally, programs that address the needs of at-risk youth and juvenile status offenders provide a cost-effective and successful approach to delinquency prevention and intervention and help ensure future public safety.

Integrated prevention and intervention programs should be initiated early in a child's development, must be culturally appropriate, and must target multiple risk factors for delinquency. . . .

Effective strategies combine programs such as truancy reduction, mentoring, conflict resolution, afterschool tutoring, vocational training, cultural development, recreation, and youth leadership in multipurpose family resource and neighborhood centers in school and community settings. . . .

Objective 5. Break the cycle of violence by addressing youth victimization, abuse, and neglect.
Many violent juveniles have themselves been victims of neglect, abuse, and violence. There is a clear link between violence in the home and a juvenile's later involvement in violent delinquency.

The Action Plan proposes strengthening three priority areas to help communities interrupt the cycle of violence. First, it advocates strengthening families' capabilities to supervise and nurture the positive development of their children in nonviolent homes and communities. Family strengthening programs can provide support through assistance with effective parenting skills, home visitation, and teen-parent groups designed to prevent child abuse and neglect and to foster healthy development.

Second, if family strengthening efforts fail and abuse and neglect occur, juvenile and family courts can play a critical role in identifying cases of child abuse and neglect, making referrals to supportive services, and providing followup. To be effective, child protective service and dependency court personnel must be well trained and have manageable caseloads. They must also be equipped with sensitive intake protocols that allow them to identify abuse and neglect cases, thoroughly investigate them, and provide prompt and appropriate services.

Third, for children at substantial risk for continued familial abuse and neglect, the Action Plan recommends stable, high-quality foster care to prevent further victimization. Equally importantly, it calls for timely planning for permanent placement or reunification to avoid multiple placements during a child's formative years. . . .

Objective 6. Strengthen and mobilize communities.
Juvenile violence stems in large part from a breakdown of family and community structures. Every community has the capacity and resources to address this breakdown by nurturing strong families, providing social support systems, and reinforcing healthy cultural norms and values. Too often, however, services are not developed, coordinated, or integrated to support these resources, leading to frustration and ineffective efforts to build positive community institutions.

Mobilizing and strengthening communities means enabling residents to recognize and solve their own problems and creating opportunities for everyone to take responsibility for finding solutions. Effective problem-solving requires involvement by adults and youth, working in partnership with local service providers, to assess problems and set priorities and to ensure that scarce energies and resources are used wisely.

A communitywide approach to reducing youth violence and delinquency is promising for two reasons. First, it affects the entire social environment by focusing on community norms, values, and policies as well as on conditions that place children at risk for adolescent problems. Second, all members of the community can apply their expertise where it is most effective. Community mobilization holds the promise of investing every local resident in solving what is truly a shared goal: helping young people grow up to maximize their potential and reduce their likelihood of involvement in violence and delinquency. Federal and State governments can assist communities by showing them the most effective ways to tap into fiscal and human resources. . . .

Objective 7. Support the development of innovative approaches to research and evaluation. . . .

Objective 8. Implement an aggressive public outreach campaign on effective strategies to combat juvenile violence.
A well-designed public information campaign is essential to the success of any juvenile violence reduction plan. The Action Plan advocates a national and local partnership with the media to mount a public information campaign designed to persuade young people to avoid violence and dangerous lifestyles, to teach adults about proven anti-violence strategies, and to involve all segments of the community in the fight against juvenile violence. The Action Plan also supports an aggressive media campaign that will help juvenile justice system and social service professionals be more effective. Communicating the types of actions that work in addressing juvenile violence to a wide variety of audiences will motivate community leaders and residents to work collaboratively.

Coordinating Council on Juvenile Justice and Delinquency Prevention, "Combating Violence and Delinquency: The National Juvenile Justice Action Plan Summary," March 1996. On-line. Internet. Available http://www.ncjrs.org/txtfiles/jjplansm.txt.

Document 11: Transferring Youths to Adult Court Is Counterproductive

The Campaign for an Effective Crime Policy contends that the increasingly popular policy of transferring juveniles to adult court fails to reduce juvenile crime and puts teens at risk of harm.

States have increasingly "toughened" statutes governing transfer of young offenders from juvenile court to adult court. Many have increased the use of transfers, and permitted transfer at younger ages and for a broader range of offenses. This approach is portrayed as sending a message to adolescents that they will face harsher punishment for serious crime, thus deterring some from engaging in criminal activity. Incarcerating young offenders in adult prisons is also intended to reduce the future toll of violent crime. . . .

A study of Florida's system indicates that transfer of juveniles into adult courts may exacerbate rather than reduce recidivism. Comparing 2,738 matched pairs of transferred and nontransferred offenders, Donna Bishop et al. found that 30 percent of youths waived into adult court were rearrested between the time of case closure and the end of the next calendar year, compared to 19 percent of the youths who remained in the juvenile system. Further, transferred juveniles were likely to reoffend more quickly than their non-waived counterparts, and their new offenses were more likely to be felonies. The authors suggest that while the transferred juveniles were more likely to be incarcerated and to serve longer sentences than youth who remained in the juvenile system, their reoffense patterns negated any incapacitative benefits that might enhance public safety. . . .

The placement of children tried as adults in adult jails and prisons has resulted in instances of sexual abuse and murder by adult inmates. To date, juveniles in adult institutions have been found to be five times more likely to be sexually assaulted, twice as likely to be beaten by staff, and 50% more likely to be attacked with a weapon than those in a juvenile facility.

The premise that children are not little adults and should not be treated as adults was the basis for establishing the juvenile court almost a century ago. Traditional roles of the juvenile court include protection of the community, constructive punishment, accountability, rehabilitation and development of competency that enable children to become contributing members of society.

Campaign for an Effective Crime Policy, *The Violent Juvenile Offender: Policy Perspectives*. Washington, DC: Campaign for an Effective Crime Policy, July 1996.

Document 12: A Brief History of the Juvenile Justice System

Lane Nelson, a staff writer for the Angolite, *the magazine of the Louisiana State Penitentiary in Angola, describes the evolution of the juvenile justice system. He concludes that the recent trend toward treating juveniles as adults is reminiscent of an earlier, less humane era.*

There was no separate judicial system for youth during the early 1800s. Everyone fell under the adult criminal code. Boys who committed crimes received the same punishment as hardened adult criminals—prison, whippings and even death. From this punishing era sprang the Child-Savers.

Child-Savers were upper-class citizens, mostly white women, who banded together for the well-being of disadvantaged and troubled youth. They became a strong political group that forced change. Some historians think Child-Savers caused as much harm as good. Anthony Platt, in his book, *The Child Savers*, states: "[T]heir attitudes toward delinquent youth were largely parentalistic and romantic but their commands were backed up by force. . . . They prompted correctional programs requiring longer terms of imprisonment, longer periods of labor, militaristic discipline, and the inoculation of middle-class values and lower-class skills."

However one views the Child-Savers, they did mark a turning point in the treatment of juvenile delinquents. Child-Savers recognized that kids were different from adults. "The present plan of promiscuous intercourse," complained Child-Saver John Pintard referring to imprisoning children and adults together, "makes little devils into great ones and at the expiration of their terms turns out accomplished villains."

Child-Savers initiated separate institutionalization for juveniles. In 1825 the first juvenile facility in America opened its doors: New York's House of Refuge. The model detention facility promised to reform wayward youth in a family-like environment, but it was operated by prison personnel used to handling adult prisoners. It functioned like a prison, although it confined mostly children who had not committed crimes. They were runaways, incorrigibles and truants who were required to do piecework for local manufacturers, or work in the community.

Despite criticism over harsh conditions in the House of Refuge, separate juvenile incarceration in so-called "reform" schools caught on. Massachusetts' Lyman for Boys Reform School opened in 1846. Three years later New York's State Agricultural and Industrial School opened and, in 1853, Maine opened its Boy's Training School. By 1900, 36 states had reform school, most of them overcrowded. The label "reformatory" was a misnomer. Juvenile prisons were punitive in nature, and children were subjected to whippings and isolation for even the slightest misbehavior.

With separate facilities in place for juvenile delinquents, the idea of a separate court system came to mind. Social worker Jane Addams is credited with the idea and passage of the Illinois Juvenile Court Act of 1899, establishing in Chicago the nation's first juvenile court. Addams envisioned and promoted a judicial system much different from the adult system. She designed it to be civil rather than criminal, predicated on the old English doctrine of *parens patriae*: the state as parent. Judges functioned like doctors prescribing treatment. As one historian notes, "[they were] parentalistic rather than adversary in nature."

By 1917, juvenile courts were established in all but three states. At the outset it was believed that a separate court system for children and the doctrine of *parens patriae* would lower juvenile incarceration rates, but that did not happen. Reform schools, now called "training" schools, were the favorite sentencing tool for most juvenile courts. Admission rates to reformatories rose between 1923 and 1933 from 15.5 to 20.2 per 100,000. The court system was based on treatment, but overcrowded reformatories were punitive. Typical "treatment" included chaining children to the wall and lashing them with a cat-o'-nine tails. The two were at cross purposes, and resulted in more rather than less delinquency. Training schools were just that, a place young males trained to become harder, craftier criminals.

Things remained pretty much the same in juvenile corrections until the 1960s. Then, through a series of rulings handed down by the U.S. Supreme Court, juveniles going through the legal process were provided due process rights. The doctrine of *parens patriae* was pushed to the side, as children were brought under a canopy of adultlike legal protections. They now had the opportunity to speak to a lawyer and defend themselves in court. With the installation of adult legal protections came the tendency to hold youth to an adult standard for the crimes they committed, and to punish them accordingly. Ironically, this "progressive" reform took the system backwards to before the Child-Savers movement, when children were also punished like adults.

Lane Nelson, "Kids Are Different," *Angolite*, July/August 1996.

Document 13: Youth Curfews in America's Cities

In 1997 the U.S. Conference of Mayors surveyed the mayors and city leaders of 347 cities regarding their use of teen curfews. Below are some of their results.

Four out of five of the survey cities (276) have a nighttime youth curfew. Of these cities, 26 percent (76) also have a daytime curfew.

Nine out of 10 of the cities (247) said that enforcing a curfew is a good use of a police officer's time. Many respondents felt that curfews represented a proactive way to combat youth violence. They saw curfews as a way to involve parents, as a deterrent to future crime, and as a way to keep juveniles from being victimized. In addition, they commented that a curfew gives the police probable cause to stop someone they think is suspicious. Examples of city comments:

- *Tulsa:* There is generally no useful purpose for a juvenile to be out late at night. Enforcement of curfews serves to protect them from being victimized by the criminal element.
- *Charlotte:* This is a good tool to protect children. Most parents didn't even know their children were outside the home.

- *Jacksonville (NC):* It provides officers with "probable cause" to stop the youth.
- *Claremont:* It frees up officers' time during the curfew hours to do other police work. Kids don't go out because they know they will get in trouble.
- *Anchorage:* Parents are contacted each time a juvenile is picked up, often eliminating repeat occurrences.
- *St. Peters (MO):* It assists in providing a method of controlling juveniles when adult supervision is lacking. Less time is spent by officers in getting them off the street than responding to problems they create.
- *Toledo:* It provides officers an opportunity to intervene with potential issues before problems develop. Periodic sweeps remind the public about the law officer. Curfew enforcement has, in large part, become a part of routine enforcement.

Twenty-six cities (10 percent) did not feel that curfew enforcement is a good use of a police officer's time. They commented that police have higher priorities than chasing curfew breakers, and that there is too much paperwork involved, tying up a police officer's time when he or she should be using that time to pursue more serious offenders. Some suggested that random sweeps seem to be more effective in keeping offenders off balance, as they are never sure when the police will be around. Finally, several commented that there is nowhere to take the young people when they are picked up because many parents aren't home. Examples of city comments:

- *San Francisco:* Offenses occur before curfew hours. Therefore, the curfew is ineffective.
- *Billings:* There is no place to take the kids. Often the parents are not home.
- *Roanoke:* There is no punishment for the law. The law is on the books but there is no punishment.
- *Freeport (IL):* It ties up the police and keeps them "babysitting" all day long.
- *Richmond (CA):* Curfews treat all youth as violators. It turns off good kids and is unfair to them. . . .

Eighty-eight percent (236) of the cities said that curfew enforcement helps to make streets safer for residents. The officials commented that there is less traffic late at night; residents feel safer; it is easier to find runaways; it is harder for criminals to hide from the police during curfew hours because there are fewer people to blend in with; graffiti and vandalism are reduced; and parents are helped to feel responsible. Examples of city comments:

- *Canton:* Police find more runaways and missing juveniles, reducing the number of delinquencies.
- *Tulsa:* The criminal element has to work harder to "hide" from cops.

- *Inglewood:* It does, in fact, make it safer. There is less traffic at night.
- *Corpus Christi:* The daytime curfew has cut down on the truancy problem considerably simply because school-aged kids observed wandering the streets or in locations away from school are easily detected, and they have come to know that.

Thirty-three cities (12 percent) said that curfews have no impact on street safety, commenting that it is people over 17 who create the more serious crimes, and that they do not always enforce the curfew due to lack of funds or lack of interest. Examples of city comments:

- *Memphis:* Most evening crimes are committed by adults.
- *Chillicothe (MO):* Those over 17 are still out causing most of the trouble.
- *Tallahassee:* Several studies have indicated that curfews displace crime to other times of the day without having any real impact over the long run.

Eighty-three percent (222) of the cities said that a curfew helps to curb gang violence. City officials believe it is a tool to reach "wanna-be" gang members and keep recruitment to a minimum; it prevents gang members from gathering; it gives the police a legal reason to contact individuals or the group; it tells kids their movements are being monitored and lessens gang activities during curfew hours. They also said that curfews help the police to identify gang members and come in contact with them at an earlier stage, help to curb young peoples' activities before they become more violent, and help the police to seize the guns and drugs of gang members, thus impairing their ability to fight. Finally, the curfew helps to educate parents to the signs of gang membership and activity. Examples of city comments:

- *Moline (IL):* Gang activity stops after curfew hours begin.
- *Dearborn:* It curbs activities before they get to a more violent level.
- *Shaker Heights:* If you address inappropriate behavior, you will minimize the opportunity for it to escalate into violence. In other words, if you catch youths early it is more likely they can become valuable members of society.
- *Napa:* I have never seen a gang member who wasn't a truant first. Curbing truancy curbs gang violence.
- *Houston:* We have had an increase in drug and weapons seizures from gangs. Seizing these things lowers gangs' ability to fight.

Seventeen percent (46) of the cities said that curfews had no impact on gang-related activities. These cities said that most hardcore gang members do not pay attention to curfews; most gang activities occur before curfews go into effect; and gangs are not afraid of curfew laws because they know there will be no punishment. Examples of city comments:

- *Ogden:* Curfews do little to curb activities of hardcore gang members.
- *Rochester (MN):* Gangs aren't afraid of curfews because the punishment is little or nothing.
- *Memphis:* Most gang activities happen before curfew hours.

U.S. Conference of Mayors, *A Status Report on Youth Curfews in America's Cities: A 347-City Survey.* Washington, DC: U.S. Conference of Mayors, 1997. On-line. Internet. Available http://www.usmayors.org/uscm/wash_update/documents/curfew.htm.

APPENDIX B

Facts About Teen Violence

— One in every 220 persons between the ages of 10 and 18 was arrested for a violent crime in 1996.

— The number of teens arrested for violent crimes increased 67 percent between 1986 and 1994, then decreased 12 percent between 1994 and 1996.

— The number of juveniles arrested for murder declined 3 percent in 1994, 14 percent in 1995, and another 14 percent in 1996.

— Juveniles made up 13 percent of violent crime arrests in 1996; specifically, 8 percent of murder arrests, 12 percent of forcible rape arrests, and 12 percent of aggravated assault arrests.

— The number of female teens arrested for violent crimes increased 25 percent between 1992 and 1996.

— Females were responsible for 15 percent of violent juvenile crime arrests in 1995.

— African American teens are arrested for violent crimes at a disproportionately higher rate than white teens; in 1996, African Americans made up about 15 percent of the teenage population but were arrested for about half of violent teen crimes.

— The juvenile population is expected to rise from its 1990 level of 27.1 million to 33.8 million in 2010, sparking fears that the juvenile crime problem will worsen dramatically.

Teen Victims of Violence

— Teens were the victims of 2.6 million violent crimes in 1994, an increase of 44 percent from 1984.

— The number of juvenile murder victims increased 82 percent between 1984 and 1994.

— Between 1984 and 1994, the number of juvenile victims of gun violence tripled, while the number of juvenile victims of nongun violence remained stable.

— In 1995, 83 percent of murder victims between 13 and 18 were killed with guns.

— In 1994 African American teens were six times more likely to be murdered than white teens.

— Gun-related murder has been the leading cause of death for African American males between the ages of 15 and 19 since 1969.

Facts About Juvenile Justice

— The first juvenile court was established in Cook County, Illinois, in 1899, marking the birth of the juvenile justice system.

— Between 1985 and 1994 the number of juvenile crime cases transferred to criminal (adult) courts increased 71 percent, from 7,200 to 12,300 cases per year.

— In a 1994 *Los Angeles Times* poll, 68 percent of respondents favored treating juveniles who commit violent crimes the same as adults.

— Of 347 cities surveyed by the U. S. Conference of Mayors, 276 (70 percent) have curfew laws.

— A 1994 Time/CNN poll found that 65 percent of white adults favored a 10:00 P.M. curfew for children under 18; 79 percent of African American adults favored such a curfew.

STUDY QUESTIONS

Chapter 1

1. Viewpoint 1 starts by describing several examples of teen violence in graphic detail. Do these anecdotes make the viewpoint more compelling, or do they seem sensationalistic? Explain your answer.

2. Both Viewpoint 1 and Viewpoint 2 point out that juveniles made up 19 percent of violent crime arrests in 1996, but they draw different conclusions from this statistic. Which viewpoint uses this statistic more effectively? Why?

3. The term *super-predators* is frequently used to describe teens who commit violent crimes. Is this term an accurate way to characterize teens who commit violence without remorse? Why or why not? Do you think the term stigmatizes all teens, even those who are not violent? Explain.

4. Having read both viewpoints in this chapter, do you believe teen crime in America is a serious problem, a moderate problem, or not much of a problem? Defend your answer with three examples from the viewpoints.

Chapter 2

1. Viewpoint 1 argues that boys need the direct influence of fathers or other men in their lives to avoid involvement in gangs, crime, and violence. Do you agree? Why or why not?

2. What does Viewpoint 2 present as the true causes of teen violence? Does this viewpoint effectively refute the argument presented in Viewpoint 1? Why or why not?

3. Viewpoint 4 claims that studies merely prove a correlation between media violence and real-world violence, not that media violence causes such violence. Do you find this argument convincing? Why or why not?

4. Do you think gangsta rap promotes violence or merely reflects the violent realities of life in the inner city?

Chapter 3

1. Based on your reading of Viewpoints 1 through 4, do you think violent teens should be subjected to harsher punishments, including transfer to adult courts? Back up your answer with at least two references to the viewpoints.

2. How important are after-school activities such as athletic and mentoring programs in preventing teen violence? Why?

3. What is the philosophy of the juvenile justice system, as described in this chapter? Do you agree with this doctrine, or do you agree with critics who believe the system is outdated and excessively lenient? Explain your reasoning.

4. Do you believe that teen curfews unduly infringe on the rights of teens? Or are they justified as a means of keeping society (including nonviolnet teens) safe from the threat of teen violence? Defend your answer with references to the viewpoints.

Organizations to Contact

The editors have compiled the following list of organizations concerned with the issues debated in this book. The descriptions are derived from materials provided by the organizations. All have publications or information available for interested readers. The list was compiled on the date of publication of the present volume; the information provided here may change. Be aware that many organizations take several weeks or longer to respond to inquiries, so allow as much time as possible.

ABA Juvenile Justice Center

750 N. Lake Shore Dr., Chicago, IL 60611
(312) 988-5000
e-mail: juvjus@abanet.org • web address: http://www.abanet.org/crimjust/juvjus/home.html

An organization of the American Bar Association, the Juvenile Justice Center disseminates information on juvenile justice systems across the country. The center provides leadership to state and local practitioners, bar associations, judges, youth workers, correctional agency staff, and policy makers. Its publications include the book *Checklist for Use in Juvenile Delinquency Proceedings*, the report *A Call for Justice: An Assessment of Access to Counsel and Quality of Representation in Delinquency Proceedings*, and the quarterly *Criminal Justice Magazine*.

American Civil Liberties Union (ACLU)

125 Broad St., 18th Fl., New York, NY 10004-2400
(212) 549-2500
e-mail: aclu@aclu.org • web address: http://www.aclu.org

The ACLU is a national organization that works to defend Americans' civil rights guaranteed by the U.S. Constitution. It opposes curfew laws for juveniles and others and seeks to protect the public assembly rights of gang members. It also opposes censoring media violence. The ACLU publishes and distributes policy statements, pamphlets, and the semiannual newsletter *Civil Liberties Alert*.

Campaign for an Effective Crime Policy (CECP)

918 F St., Suite 501, Washington, DC 20004
(202) 628-0871 • fax: (202) 628-1091
e-mail: staff @sproject.com • web address: http://www.sproject.com/
home.htm (temporary host website until CECP sets up its own)

CECP's purpose is to promote information, ideas, discussion, and
debate about criminal justice policy and to advocate alternative sentencing policies. The campaign's core document, available to the
public, is the book *A Call for Rational Debate on Crime and Punishment.*

Children's Defense Fund (CDF)

25 E St. NW, Washington, DC 20001
(202) 628-8787
e-mail: cdfinfo@childrensdefense.org • web address: http://www.
childrensdefense.org

The Children's Defense Fund advocates policies and programs to
improve the lives of children and teens in America. CDF's Safe Start
program works to prevent the spread of violence and guns in
schools. The fund publishes the monthly newsletter *CDF Reports,*
on-line news and reports such as *Children in the States: 1998 Data*
and *How to Reduce Teen Violence,* and *The State of America's Children,*
an annual yearbook that contains various articles and papers concerning the children of America.

National Center on Institutions and Alternatives (NCIA)

3125 Mt. Vernon Ave., Alexandria, VA 22305
(703) 684-0373 • fax: (703) 684-6037
e-mail: ncia@igc.apc.org • web address: http://www.ncianet.org/ncia

NCIA works to reduce the number of people institutionalized in
prisons and mental hospitals. It favors the least restrictive forms of
detention for juvenile offenders, and it opposes sentencing juveniles
as adults and executing juvenile murderers. NCIA publishes the
monthly *Augustus: A Journal of Progressive Human Services,* the book
Youth Homicide: Keeping Perspective on How Many Children Kill, 1997,
and *Scared Straight: A Second Look.*

National Council on Crime and Delinquency (NCCD)

685 Market St., Suite 620, San Francisco, CA 94105
(415) 896-6223 • fax: (415) 896-5109
e-mail: pat@nccdsf.attmail.com • web address: http://www.nccd.com

NCCD comprises corrections specialists and others interested in the juvenile justice system and the prevention of crime and delinquency. It advocates community-based treatment programs rather than imprisonment for delinquent youths. It opposes placing minors in adult jails and executing those who have committed capital offenses before age eighteen. It publishes the quarterlies *Crime and Delinquency* and the *Journal of Research in Crime and Delinquency* as well as policy papers, including the "Juvenile Justice Policy Statement" and "Unlocking Juvenile Corrections: Evaluating the Massachusetts Department of Youth Services."

National Crime Prevention Council (NCPC)

1700 K St. NW, 2nd Fl., Washington, DC 20006-3817
(202) 466-6272 • fax: (202) 296-1356
e-mail: tcc@ncpc.org • web address: http://www.ncpc.org/

NCPC provides training and technical assistance to groups and individuals interested in crime prevention. It advocates job training and recreation programs as means to reduce youth crime and violence. The council, which sponsors the Take a Bite Out of Crime campaign, publishes the book *Making a Difference: Young People in Community Crime Prevention*, the booklet *Making Children, Families, and Communities Safer from Violence*, and the newsletter *Catalyst*, which is published ten times a year.

National Criminal Justice Association (NCJA)

444 N. Capitol St. NW, Suite 618, Washington, DC 20001
(202) 624-1440 • fax: (202) 508-3859
e-mail: ncja@sso.org • web address: http://www.sso.org/ncja/

NCJA is an association of state and local police chiefs, judges, attorneys, and other criminal justice officials who seek to improve the administration of state criminal and juvenile justice programs. It publishes the monthly newsletter *Justice Bulletin*.

National Institute of Justice (NIJ)

PO Box 6000, Rockville, MD 20849-6000
(800) 851-3420 • (301) 519-5500
e-mail: askncjrs@ncjrs.org • web address: http://www.ojp.usdoj.gov/nij/

NIJ is a research and development agency that documents crime and its control. It publishes and distributes its information through the National Criminal Justice Reference Service, an international clearinghouse that provides information and research about criminal justice. Its publications include the research briefs *Criminal Behavior of Gang Members and At-Risk Youths, Crime in the Schools: A Problem-Solving Approach,* and *Violence Among Middle School and High School Students: Analysis and Implications for Prevention.*

Office of Juvenile Justice and Delinquency Prevention (OJJDP)

810 Seventh St. NW, 8th Fl., Washington, DC 20531
(202) 307-5911 • fax: (202) 514-6382
e-mail: garrye@ojp.usdoj.gov • web address: http://www.ncjrs.org/ojjhome.htm

As the primary federal agency charged with monitoring and improving the juvenile justice system, OJJDP develops and funds programs to advance juvenile justice. Among its goals are the prevention and control of illegal drug use and serious juvenile crime. Through its National Youth Gang Clearinghouse, OJJDP investigates and focuses public attention on the problem of youth gangs. The office publishes the *OJJDP Juvenile Justice Bulletin* periodically.

Victims of Crime and Leniency (VOCAL)

PO Box 4449, Montgomery, AL 36103
(800) 239-3219 • (334) 262-7197 • fax: (334) 262-7121

VOCAL is an organization of crime victims who seek to ensure that their rights are recognized and protected. Members believe that the U.S. justice system goes to great lengths to protect the rights of criminals while discounting those of victims. VOCAL publishes the quarterly newsletter *VOCAL Voice.*

Youth Crime Watch of America (YCWA)

9300 S. Dadeland Blvd., Suite 100, Miami, FL 33156
(305) 670-2409 • fax: (305) 670-3805
e-mail: ycwa@ycwa.org • web address: http://www.ycwa.org

YCWA is dedicated to establishing Youth Crime Watch programs across the United States. It strives to give youths the tools and guidance necessary to actively reduce crime and drug use in their schools and communities. YCWA publications include a variety of resources on beginning new Youth Crime Watch programs as well as the book *Talking to Youth About Crime Prevention,* the *Community Based Youth Crime Watch Program Handbook,* and the motivational video *A Call for Young Heroes.*

FOR FURTHER READING

Renardo Barden, *Juvenile Violence*. New York: Marshall Cavendish, 1994. A good overview of the problem of violence by children and teens. Focuses on the causes of such violence at home, in society, and in schools. Also deals with racial violence and violence against women and girls.

Carl Bosch, *Schools Under Siege: Guns, Gangs, and Hidden Dangers*. Springfield, NJ: Enslow, 1997. Paints a disturbing picture of violence and environmental hazards in America's schools and describes efforts to make schools safer.

Vic Cox, *Guns, Violence, and Teens*. Springfield, NJ: Enslow, 1997. Examines the problem of gun violence by and against teens, including gun violence in the schools. Also presents the debate over gun control and describes the public health approach to combating gun violence.

Ellen Heath Grinney, *Delinquency and Criminal Behavior*. New York: Chelsea House, 1992. An overview that focuses on the history of society's treatment of juvenile delinquents, the establishment of reform schools and the juvenile justice system, the causes of delinquency, and the problems of drug abuse and gang violence.

Susan S. Lang, *Teen Violence*, rev. ed. New York: Franklin Watts, 1994. A good overview that examines the causes of teen violence and discusses the juvenile justice system, school violence, sexual violence, suicide, and how to respond to these problems.

Margot Webb, *Coping with Street Gangs*. New York: Rosen, 1992. Describes gangs and discusses why youths join them. Also offers ways individuals and society at large can deal with the gang problem.

WORKS CONSULTED

Books

Huub Angenent and Anton de Man, *Background Factors of Juvenile Delinquency*. New York: Peter Lang, 1996. A readable textbook that explores the question of what causes some young people to commit crime.

Ronald J. Berger, ed., *The Sociology of Juvenile Delinquency*. Chicago: Nelson-Hall, 1991. A collection of readings designed for upper-division college courses.

Léon Bing, *Do or Die*. New York: HarperCollins, 1991. A journalist's view of Los Angeles gang life.

Geoffrey Canada, *Fist Stick Knife Gun: A Personal History of Violence in America*. Boston: Beacon Press, 1995. Provides a firsthand account of growing up on the violent streets of the South Bronx during the 1950s and 1960s and examines the problem of inner-city youth violence today.

Shirley Dicks, ed., *Young Blood: Juvenile Justice and the Death Penalty*. Amherst, NY: Prometheus Books. A collection of essays that focus on the juvenile justice system, the practice of trying juveniles as adults, and the death penalty for juveniles.

Charles Patrick Ewing, *Kids Who Kill*. Lexington, MA: Lexington Books, 1990. Presents numerous case histories of children and teens who have committed murder and attempts to divine their motives.

James Gilligan, *Violence: Our Deadly Epidemic and Its Causes*. New York: G.P. Putnam's Sons, 1996. A discussion of the causes and prevention of violent behavior by a psychiatrist who worked with violent prisoners and the criminally insane for twenty-five years.

Peter W. Greenwood et al., *Diverting Children from a Life of Crime: Measuring Costs and Benefits*. Santa Monica, CA: RAND, 1996. Compares the cost and effectiveness of four intervention approaches with each other and with incarceraton.

Allan M. Hoffman, ed., *Schools, Violence, and Society*. Westport, CT: Praeger, 1996. A collection of scholarly essays that examine the problem of school violence in depth, including its causes and potential solutions.

James C. Howell et al., eds., *Sourcebook on Serious, Violent, and Chronic Juvenile Offenders*. Thousand Oaks, CA: Sage, 1995. An anthology of scholarly writings on strategies to address the problem of violent juvenile crime.

Robin Karr-Morse and Meredith S. Wiley, *Ghosts from the Nursery: Tracing the Roots of Violence*. New York: Atlantic Monthly Press, 1997. Examines how abuse, neglect, and environmental stresses in the womb and during the first two years of life can lead to violent behavior in later years.

Malcolm W. Klein, *The American Street Gang: Its Nature, Prevalence, and Control*. New York: Oxford University Press, 1995. A scholarly discussion of gangs that focuses in part on the nature and prevalence of gang violence.

Richard J. Lundman, *Prevention and Control of Juvenile Delinquency*, 2nd ed. New York: Oxford University Press, 1993. Provides an overview of delinquency prevention strategies and focuses on particularly important projects.

Deborah Porothrow-Stith, with Michaele Weissman, *Deadly Consequences*. New York: HarperCollins, 1991. Discusses the causes and consequences of youth violence and presents the authors' proposal to address this problem with a public health strategy that emphasizes prevention.

Barbara F. Reskin and Irene Padavic, *Women and Men at Work*. Thousand Oaks, CA: Pine Forge Press, 1994. An examination of gender inequality and discrimination against women in the workplace.

Ira M. Schwartz, ed., *Juvenile Justice and Public Policy: Toward a National Agenda*. New York: Lexington Books, 1992. A compilation of writings that focus on various aspects of juvenile justice policy.

Ira M. Schwartz and William H. Barton, eds., *Reforming Juvenile Detention: No More Hidden Closets*. Columbus: Ohio University Press, 1994. A collection of essays that detail the problems of the juvenile detention system and offer recommendations for reform.

Joseph F. Sheley and James D. Wright, *In the Line of Fire: Youth, Guns, and Violence in Urban America*. New York: Aldine de Gruyter, 1995. A study of gun possession by adolescents in five inner cities, focusing on how many own guns and why they carry them.

Donald J. Shoemaker, *Theories of Delinquency: An Examination of Delinquent Behavior.* New York: Oxford University Press, 1996. A survey of various theoretical approaches to understanding the causes of delinquent behavior.

James F. Short, *Delinquency and Society.* Englewood Cliffs, NJ: Prentice Hall, 1990. A challenging sociology textbook on juvenile delinquency; provides some theoretical and historical context for the study of teen violence.

Gini Sikes, *8 Ball Chicks.* New York: Doubleday, 1997. An examination of girl gangs in several U.S. cities by a seasoned journalist who spent a year among them.

Irving A. Spergel, *The Youth Gang Problem: A Community Approach.* New York: Oxford University Press, 1995. An in-depth analysis of gangs that challenges the common assumptions regarding the relationship between gangs, drug trafficking, and gang violence.

Periodicals and Websites

American Academy of Pediatrics, "Media Violence," *Pediatrics,* June 1995.

American Civil Liberties Union, "ACLU Fact Sheet on Juvenile Crime," *In Congress,* May 14, 1996. On-line. Internet. Available http://www.aclu.org/congress/juvenile.htm.

American Civil Liberties Union, "ACLU Fact Sheet on the Juvenile Justice System," July 1996. On-line. Internet. Available http://www.aclu.org/library/fctsht.html.

American Civil Liberties Union, "Curfew Overturned in Washington State," press release, June 2, 1997. On-line. Internet. Available http://www.aclu-wa.org/pubs/releases/970602.shtml.

American Psychological Association, "Violence on Television: What Do Children Learn? What Can Parents Do?" 1998. On-line. Internet. Available http://www.apa.org/pubinfo/violence.html.

David C. Anderson, "When Should Kids Go to Jail?" *American Prospect,* May/June 1998.

Charles Augustus Ballard, "Prodigal Dad: How We Bring Fathers Home to Their Children," *Policy Review,* Winter 1995.

William J. Bennett, testimony before the House Ways and Means Committee, Subcommittee on Human Resources, January 20, 1995.

Shay Bilchik, "Saving America's Children—a Little at the Time," *San Diego Union-Tribune*, September 18, 1997.

Donna M. Bishop et al., "The Transfer of Juveniles to Criminal Court: Does It Make a Difference?" *Crime & Delinquency*, April 1996.

George Brooks, "Let's Not Gang Up on Kids," *U.S. Catholic*, March 1997.

Michael P. Brown, "Juvenile Offenders: Should They Be Tried in Adult Courts?" *USA Today*, January 1998.

Fox Butterfield, "With Juvenile Courts in Chaos, Critics Propose Their Demise," *New York Times*, July 21, 1997.

Sidney Callahan, "What We See, We Do," *Commonweal*, January 12, 1996.

Children's Defense Fund, "Juvenile Crime Bill Would Harm Children," *Action Alert!* January 15, 1997. On-line. Internet. Available http://www.childrensdefense.org/s10.html.

William Claiborne, "Bombs Found in Ore. Teen's Home," *Washington Post*, May 23, 1998. On-line. Internet. Available http://www.washingtonpost.com/wp-srv/national/lonterm/juvmurders/stories/bombs.htm.

CNN Interactive, "Who Is Michael Carneal?" December 3, 1997. On-line. Internet. Available http://www.cnn.com/US/9712/03/school.shooting.pm/.

Roger L. Conner, "A Gangsta's Rights," *Responsive Community*, Winter 1995–1996.

CQ Researcher, "Preventing Juvenile Crime: Is Tougher Punishment or Prevention the Answer?" March 15, 1996.

John J. DiIulio Jr., "Defining Criminality Up," *Wall Street Journal*, July 3, 1996.

———, statement before the U.S. Senate Subcommittee on Youth Violence, February 28, 1996.

———, "Stop Crime Where It Starts," *New York Times*, July 31, 1996.

Kevin Durkin, "Chasing the Effects of Media Violence," *ABA Update: Newsletter of the Australian Broadcasting Authority*, March 1995. On-line. Internet. Available http://www.screen.com/mnet/eng/issues/violence/resource/articles/chasefx.htm.

Barbara Ehrenreich, "Oh, Grow Up!" *Time*, November 4, 1996.

Delbert S. Elliott, "Youth Violence: An Overview," working paper, Center for the Study of Youth Policy, University of Pennsylvania, Philadelphia, 1993.

Christopher John Farley and James Willwerth, "Dead Teen Walking," *Time*, January 19, 1998.

Suzanne Fields, "Teenage Mischief Becomes Teenage Terror, *Conservative Chronicle*, November 17, 1993.

James Alan Fox, "Should the Federal Government Have a Major Role in Reducing Juvenile Crime? Pro," *Congressional Digest*, August/September 1996.

Jonathan Freedman, "Violence in the Mass Media and Violence in Society: The Link Is Unproven," *Harvard Mental Health Letter*, May 1996.

T. Markus Funk, "Young and Arrestless," *Reason*, February 1996.

Evan Gahr, "Towns Turn Teens into Pumpkins," *Insight*, February 3, 1997.

David Gergen, "Taming Teenage Wolf Packs," *U.S. News & World Report*, March 25, 1996.

Ted Gest and Victoria Pope, "Crime Time Bomb," *U.S. News & World Report*, March 25, 1996.

Georgie Anne Geyer, "'Gun-Crazy,' Yes, but the Causes of Teen Shootings Run Much Deeper," *San Diego Union-Tribune*, May 31, 1998.

Todd Gitlin, "Imagebusters: The Hollow Crusade Against TV Violence," *American Prospect*, Winter 1994.

Gloria Goodale, "Battles over Media Violence Move to a New Frontier: The Internet," *Christian Science Monitor*, November 18, 1996.

———, "Safeguarding the Children," *Christian Science Monitor*, November 18, 1996.

Sandy Grady, "The Questions After Jonesboro," *San Diego Union-Tribune*, March 27, 1998.

Jean Baldwin Grossman and Eileen M. Garry, "Mentoring—A Proven Delinquency Prevention Strategy," *Juvenile Justice Bulletin*, April 1997.

David Heim, "American Mayhem," *Christian Century*, June 3–10, 1998.

James C. Howell, "Abolish the Juvenile Court? Nonsense!" *Juvenile Justice Update*, February/March 1998.

Dan Hurley, "They Said It Couldn't Happen Here," *Family Circle*, April 26, 1994.

Sarah Ingersoll, "The National Juvenile Justice Action Plan: A Comprehensive Response to a Critical Challenge," *Journal of the Office of Juvenile Justice and Delinquency Prevention*, September 1997.

Michelle Ingrassia, "'Life Means Nothing,'" *Newsweek*, July 19, 1993.

Issues and Controversies On File, "Teen Curfews," August 30, 1996.

———, "Teen Gangs and Crime," February 9, 1996.

Laurence Jarvik, "Violence in Pursuit of Justice Is No Vice," *Insight*, December 19, 1994.

Elizabeth Kastor, "What Makes Children Kill?" *Washington Post*, March 27, 1998.

John Kifner, "From Wild Talk and Friendship to Five Deaths in a Schoolyard," *New York Times*, March 29, 1998.

Patricia King and Andrew Murr, "A Son Who Spun Out of Control," *Newsweek*, June 1, 1998.

Richard Lacayo, "Lock 'Em Up!" *Time*, February 7, 1994.

———, "Teen Crime," *Time*, July 21, 1997.

———, "Toward the Root of the Evil," *Time*, April 6, 1998.

Matt Lait, "Study Finds Curfew Law Fails to Curb Violent Crime," *Los Angeles Times*, February 10, 1998.

John Leonard, "Why Blame TV?" *Utne Reader*, May/June 1994.

S. Robert Lichter, "Bam! Whoosh! Crack! TV Worth Squelching," *Insight*, December 19, 1994.

Michael A. Males, "Executioner's Myth," *Los Angeles Times*, May 4, 1997.

———, "The Truth About Crime: Myth of Teenage Violence vs. Real Adult Menace," *Los Angeles Times*, September 15, 1996.

Mike Males, "Bashing Youth: Media Myths About Teenagers," *Extra!* March/April 1994.

————, "Wild in Deceit: Why 'Teen Violence' Is Poverty Violence in Disguise," *Extra!* March/April 1996.

Mike Males and Faye Docuyanan, "Crackdown on Kids: Giving Up on the Young," *Progressive*, February 1996.

Nathan McCall, "My Rap Against Rap," *Washington Post*, November 14, 1993.

Sara S. McLanahan, "The Consequences of Single Motherhood," *American Prospect*, Summer 1994.

Mediascope, "Video Game Violence" Issue Brief, n.d. On-line. Internet. Available http://www.igc.apc.org/mediascope/fvidviol. htm.

Kristine Napier, "Antidotes to Pop Culture Poison," *Policy Review*, November/December 1997.

National Television Violence Study, 1994-1995, "Summary of Findings and Recommendations." On-line. Internet. Available http:// www.mediascope.org/medias.

Kim Nauer, "Motive and Opportunity," *City Limits*, December 1995.

Teresa Nelson, ACLU press release, April 10, 1996. On-line. Internet. Available http://www.aclu.org/news.n041096.html.

Christina Nifong, "Teens Learn to Walk away from Dating Violence," *Christian Science Monitor*, December 16, 1996.

Patrick O'Neill, "Teen Killers Do Fit a Pattern, Experts Say," *San Diego Union-Tribune*, May 31, 1998.

Clarence Page, "B.I.G. Problems at the Root of Rap Violence," *Liberal Opinion Week*, March 24, 1997.

————, "Consensus Reflects a Changing 'Family,'" *Liberal Opinion Week*, August 8, 1994.

Margot Prior, speech presented at the Stories We Tell Our Children Conference in Melbourne, Australia, August 1994. On-line. Internet. Available http://cii2.cochran.com/mnet/eng/ issues/violence/resource/docs/C-aba-ag.htm.

Robert Rector, "Welfare Reform," *Issues '96: The Candidate's Briefing Book*. Washington, DC: The Heritage Foundation, 1996.

Morgan Reynolds, "Abolish the Juvenile Justice System?" *Intellectual Ammunition*, November/December 1996. On-line. Internet. Available http://www.heartland.org/03nvdc96.htm.

Tricia Rose, "Rap Music and the Demonization of Young Black Males," *USA Today*, May 1994.

Byron M. Roth, "Crime and Child-Rearing: What Can Public Policy Do?" *Current*, January 1997.

William Ruefle and Kenneth Mike Reynolds, "Curfews and Delinquency in Major American Cities," *Crime & Delinquency*, July 1995.

Bruce Shapiro, "The Adolescent Lockup," *Nation*, July 7, 1997.

Robert E. Shepherd Jr., "The Proliferation of Juvenile Curfews," American Bar Association Criminal Justice Section, Juvenile Justice Center, n.d. On-line. Internet. Available http://www.abanet.org/crimjust/juvjust/cjcurfew.html.

Nina Shokraii, "Congress Must Act to Protect Parents' Rights," *Insight*, May 20, 1996.

Arlene Skolnick and Stacey Rosencranz, "The New Crusade for the Old Family," *American Prospect*, Summer 1994.

Howard N. Snyder, "Juvenile Arrests: 1996," *Juvenile Justice Bulletin*, November 1997.

"Speakers' Three Strikes for Juvenile, Boot Camp Bills Move Forward," press release, Office of Cruz M. Bustamente, April 22, 1997. On-line. Internet. Available http://www.assembly.ca.gov/demweb/members/a31/press/p3197019.htm

Michael Tanner, testimony before the Senate Judiciary Committee, Subcommittee on Youth Violence, June 7, 1995.

Don Terry, "Sentences for Boy Killers Renew Debate on Saving Society's Lost," *New York Times*, January 31, 1996.

Time Daily, "The Curfew Card," May 31, 1996. On-line. Internet. Available http://cgi.pathfinder.com/time/daily/article/0,1344,6712,00.html.

USA Today, "Violence Triggers a Vicious Cycle," December 1995.

Nancy Watzman, "The Curfew Revival Gains Momentum," *Governing*, Fall 1994.

Woody West, "A Slap on the Wrist for 'Naughty' Kids," *Insight*, August 19, 1996.

Timothy Wheeler, "Blaming the Guns," *Washington Times*, June 2, 1998. On-line. Internet. Available http://www.claremont.org/wheeler2.htm.

Barbara Dafoe Whitehead, "Dan Quayle Was Right," *Atlantic Monthly*, April 1993.

Gordon Witkin et al., "Again," *U.S. News & World Report*, June 1, 1998.

Robert L. Woodson, "Reclaiming the Lives of Young People," *USA Today*, September 1997.

James Wootton and Robert O. Heck, "How State and Local Officials Can Combat Violent Juvenile Crime," *Heritage Foundation Backgrounder*, October 28, 1996.

Mortimer B. Zuckerman, "Forrest Gump vs. Ice-T," *U.S. News & World Report*, July 24, 1995.

Reports

Alfred Blumstein, *Youth Violence, Guns, and Illicit Drug Markets*. Washington, DC: National Institute of Justice, June 1996.

Children's Defense Fund, *The State of America's Children: Yearbook 1997*. Washington, DC: Children's Defense Fund, 1997.

Coalition for Juvenile Justice, *No Easy Answers: Juvenile Justice in a Climate of Fear*. Washington, DC: Coalition for Juvenile Justice, 1995.

Barbara Tatem Kelley et al., *Epidemiology of Serious Violence*. Washington, DC: Office of Juvenile Justice and Delinquency Prevention, June 1997.

Barry Krisberg, *The Impact of the Justice System on Serious, Violent, and Chronic Juvenile Offenders*. San Francisco: National Council on Crime and Delinquency, May 1997.

Cheryl L. Maxson, *Street Gangs and Drug Sales in Two Suburban Cities*. Washington, DC: National Institute of Justice, September 1995.

Office of Juvenile Justice and Delinquency Prevention, *Comprehensive Strategy for Serious, Violent, and Chronic Juvenile Offenders: Program Summary*. Washington, DC: Office of Juvenile Justice and Delinquency Prevention, 1994.

U.S. Conference of Mayors, *A Status Report on Youth Curfews in America's Cities: A 347-City Survey*. Washington, DC: United States Conference of Mayors, 1997.

Kevin N. Wright and Karen E. Wright, *Family Life, Delinquency, and Crime: A Policymaker's Guide*. Washington, DC: Office of Juvenile Justice and Delinquency Prevention, May 1994.

INDEX

ABOUT THE AUTHOR

Scott Barbour has worked as a book editor, senior editor, and managing editor at Greenhaven Press. He continues to work for Greenhaven on a freelance basis as he pursues a master's degree in social work.